From 1790 to 1860 the southern United States became one of the mightiest slave empires in the known history of the world.

As the sun rose it summoned millions of black workers to their unpaid toil; when it sank many hours later the same millions were still at work. Day after day these people mingled their anguish with struggle. Tools were damaged, buildings set on fire. Occasionally there was murder, suicide, armed rebellion; and often, there was desperate flight.

Black solidarity was nourished by both the struggle for survival and the forced segregation that was part of slavery. Out of this separate and shared experience emerged a unique and new black American culture.

Slowly at first, then with increasing militancy, white people joined with black in the antislavery movement. Moderates sought to unite northerners in setting limits on the advance of slavery into the western territories. Radicals championed a new concept of American citizenship in which all people, regardless of the color of their skin, would enjoy the same freedom and the same legal rights.

Through contemporary accounts, including reports by the slaves themselves, Mr. Scott gives a vivid picture of life in the slave South and of the antislavery struggle which that life inevitably created and nourished.

The Living History Library

General Editor: John Anthony Scott

Hard Trials on My Way

Slavery and the Struggle Against It

★ **1800-1860** ★

John Anthony Scott

Illustrated with contemporary prints and photographs

ALFRED A. KNOPF: NEW YORK

THIS IS A BORZOI BOOK PUBLISHED BY ALFRED A. KNOPF, INC.

Copyright © 1974 by John Anthony Scott.
All rights reserved under International and Pan-American Copyright Conventions.
Published in the United States by Alfred A. Knopf, Inc., New York,
and simultaneously in Canada by Random House of Canada Limited, Toronto.
Distributed by Random House, Inc., New York.

Library of Congress Cataloging in Publication Data
Scott, John Anthony, 1916–. Hard trials on my way. (Living history library)
Summary: An account of life in the slave South, and the
anti-slavery struggle which that life created. Includes Nat Turner,
Henry Bibb, Elijah Lovejoy, John Brown, and many anonymous slaves.
Bibliography: 1. Slavery in the United States—Juvenile literature.
2. Slavery in the United States—Anti-slavery movements—Juvenile literature.
[1. Slavery in the United States] I. Title. E441.S37 1974 322.4′4′0973
74-7395   ISBN 0-394-82045-2   ISBN 0-394-92045-7 (lib. bdg.)

Manufactured in the United States of America. 0 9 8 7 6 5 4 3 2 1

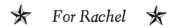 *For Rachel*

CONTENTS

Introduction

INTRODUCTION

Slavery existed in the North American colonies of Great Britain and in the United States for more than two hundred years. Much of that time it was part of the fabric of American life not only in the South but throughout the North as well. It reached the height of its power during the period from 1800 to 1860, with which this book deals. In this period, too, the struggle against slavery was coherently organized and moved rapidly toward its climax in the Civil War. This antislavery struggle was begun, and initially carried on, by slaves themselves. In the course of time it engulfed the whole nation.

The struggle against slavery is a central and enduring heritage of the slavery years. It was a tragic struggle of tremendous human dignity; it began the titanic task of eliminating a cruel system which had sunk deep roots in the American soil. But its success was partial and incomplete. It was left to later generations to finish what earlier ones had begun.

It is the purpose of this book to probe the meaning of slavery as defined by the actual experience of black people and by the very words with which they described that experience. Of equal concern will be the scope and meaning of the struggles into which both black and white people entered to record their protest and their defiance.

The study of slavery is no mere academic exercise. Twentieth-century Americans urgently need to understand the experience of slavery in order to continue the struggle to root up what is left of it in our own time.

But it is not possible to wipe out what survives of slavery without, at the same time, creating an interracial society where people of many different ethnic identities are cherished, not because they are the same, but because they are gloriously different. The study of slavery is not only necessary for those, both black and white, who want to emancipate themselves from the past; it is also a necessary step in creating a new, rainbow-hued vision of the American future.

Hard Trials on My Way

THE BLACK CLOUD
Slavery Moves South, 1787–1840

I stood entranced as the noble creature swept, like a black cloud, over the river, his bald white head bent forward and shining in the sun, and his fierce eyes and beak directed toward one of the beautiful wild ducks on the water, which he had evidently marked for his prey.

Frances Anne Kemble, *Journal of a Residence on a Georgian Plantation*

In May 1787 Major Pierce Butler reached New York with his wife, Polly, and his family after a long sea trip from South Carolina. The major waited long enough to see Polly and the children comfortably settled in their summer quarters, and then took ship for Philadelphia. He arrived in the capital city on May 24 to play his part, as a delegate from South Carolina, in constructing a constitution for the United States.

The Constitutional Convention sat all summer; Pierce Butler's part in its deliberations was an important one. By the end of October, when the Convention disbanded, he was exhausted by his labors but reasonably certain that they had been worthwhile. "If," he wrote to an English friend, "the Constitution meets with the approbation of the states, I shall feel myself fully recom-

pensed for my share of the trouble, and a Summer's confinement which injured my health much. . . . In passing
judgment on it you must call to mind that we had
Clashing Interests to reconcile—some strong prejudices
to encounter. . . ."

Major Pierce Butler was one of the founders of the
United States, and he was also one of the country's
biggest slaveholders. Butler had come to America in 1766
as an officer in the British Army. He liked the country,
and decided to settle. His marriage to Polly Middleton,
a South Carolina heiress, made him a wealthy man, and
in time he became the father of one son and four daughters. In 1776 Butler had joined up with the revolutionaries. Here he was now, in 1787, a delegate to the Constitutional Convention from the state of South Carolina.

Butler made many important contributions to the
debates that were held in the stifling atmosphere of Constitution Hall. He argued, for example, that the southern
states should have representatives in the House of Representatives proportional to their total population, free
and slave: "The labor of a slave in South Carolina," he
insisted, "is as valuable and productive as that of a freeman in Massachusetts . . . an equal representation ought
to be allowed for them in a government which was in-
stituted principally for the protection of property, and
was itself to be supported by property."

Butler was arguing in effect that *slaveholders* should
have more political punch in Congress than freemen—
no one, obviously, was going to allow *slaves* either to
vote or to get elected. Butler's plan was strenuously
opposed by delegates from the North; it would give,
they pointed out, a disproportionate representation to

the southern slaveholding states. Not so, said Butler; the South needed this power in order to guarantee that no majority of representatives from the free states would pass a law to abolish slavery. "The security the Southern states want," said he, "is that their negroes may not be taken from them, which some gentlemen . . . have a very good mind to do."

Butler, then, was a leader of what he himself called the Slavery Interest. He, rather than George Washington or Thomas Jefferson, represented the thinking of a majority of the big slave owners of that day. Washington and Jefferson, as they grew older, both viewed the fact of slavery as a matter of increasing concern. Washington set all his slaves free when he died, and Jefferson in his later life talked of doing the same thing. But they, as liberal and relatively humane slave owners, were in a minority. Already in 1787, when the fine rhetoric of the Declaration of Independence was still ringing in everyone's ears, Butler and his class had a different vision of the future. Their goals were not the elimination of slavery, but its perpetuation, not the abolition of slavery, but its expansion and development.

On September 17 the Convention closed its deliberations; Pierce Butler returned to New York by packet ship to pick up his family, and then headed back South. Two years later Polly died; Butler took the family slaves and went to seek his fortune on fresh and fertile lands in Georgia.

The major was acting in response to changes in the international market. British textile manufacturers were at that time developing a bottomless appetite for raw cotton. The Sea Island coast, with its humid semitropical climate, was admirably suited for raising fine cotton for the British market; and the coastal swamps, of immense fertility, were also well suited for the production of crops like sugar and rice.

The major was only one of many Virginia and Carolina planters who moved southward at that time in search of new lands and new profits; and who took their black slaves with them to toil on the cotton lands and in the rice swamps. This fresh expansion of slavery was taking place at the very moment that the new Constitution was being created.

Between 1790 and 1800 Major Butler acquired a vast estate in the Georgia Sea Islands. He diked and cleared a huge swamp in the estuary of the Altamaha River, and named it Butler Island after himself; he also bought a tract of land at the northern edge of Saint Simons Island. Amid those watery wastes, he founded his own private empire, ruling his black servants with the ironclad discipline of an Oriental despot. By the time he died in 1822, Butler was the wealthiest planter in Georgia, and one of the wealthiest in the entire South. He built himself a princely residence at Hampton Point —for that was the name of the Saint Simons Island property—and a fine winter house on Chestnut Street in Philadelphia. All his daughters settled in Philadelphia and made that city, not the South, their home.

At his death Butler owned about seven hundred slaves who toiled on the Georgia estate under the direction of an overseer, or estate manager. What kind of life did the black people lead there?

The story of Major Butler's Sea Island slaves has been told by his grandson's wife, Fanny Kemble. Fanny was

Fanny Kemble, by Thomas Sully.

a famous British actress who toured the United States in 1832. After playing to New York audiences for a couple of months, she went to Philadelphia and performed at the Old Drury Theater, a couple of blocks from the Butlers' Chestnut Street home. Pierce Butler, grandson of the major, was living there at the time with his maiden aunts, Frances and Elizabeth. He went to see Fanny act, became one of her fans, called upon her at her hotel, took her riding, and so on. The couple was married in 1834 at Philadelphia's Trinity Church.

At the end of 1838, Fanny made her first and only visit to the Georgia plantations her husband and his brother John inherited in 1836 on the death of their Aunt Frances. Fanny spent a little over three months on the Sea Island coast—half the time on Butler Island, half on Saint Simons. Deeply moved by the beauty of the country and by the agonies that its black people endured, Fanny kept a journal of her experiences and observations. This was published a quarter of a century later, in the middle of the Civil War. It was written by a brilliant woman who detested slavery and who was endowed with a keen sensitivity to human life and human sorrow. The journal was the record of one talented individual, but it confronts and illuminates universal truths of the slavery experience.

Mrs. Butler went first to the Butler Island plantation; this was a vast swamp in the middle of the Altamaha River which the major, by diking and draining, had converted into a rice field of great fertility. By 1839, the time of Fanny's visit, this island was the foundation of the family wealth; a slave population of nearly four hundred lived and toiled on it. The people inhabited

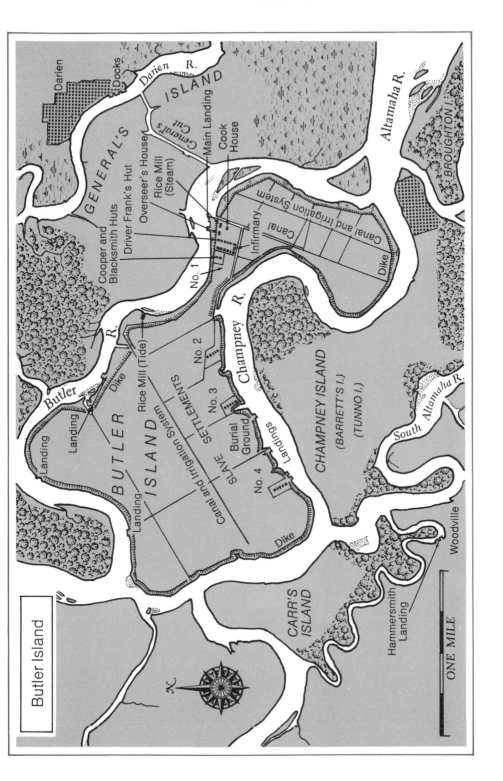

Butler Island

ONE MILE

four villages, or "camps," separated from one another by a wide expanse of fields. To each village was attached a kitchen, also blacksmith and cooper shops where

all the common iron implements of husbandry or household use for the estate are made, and . . . all the rice barrels necessary for the crop, tubs and buckets, large and small, for the use of the people.

Mill engineers, blacksmiths, coopers, carpenters, and weavers were, of course, all slaves and all were highly skilled craftsmen:

There are here a gang of coopers, blacksmiths, of bricklayers, of carpenters, all well acquainted with their particular trades. [They] are not only exceedingly expert at them, but exhibit a greater general activity of intellect, which must necessarily result from even a partial degree of cultivation.

But the majority of the slaves on this or any other big plantation were field hands—toil-worn human beings, both men and women, who labored in the fields from the first trace of dawn until nightfall. It is with the life and labor of these millions of ordinary, anonymous people that the story of slavery in the United States must first and foremost be concerned.

The field hands on the Butler estate, as on all big plantations, were divided into gangs. "At the head of each gang," wrote Fanny,

is a driver who stands over them, whip in hand, while they perform their daily task, who renders an account of each individual slave and his work every evening to the overseer, and receives from him directions for their next day's tasks. Each driver is allowed to inflict a dozen lashes upon any refractory slave in the field, and at the time of the offense.

Not only were there drivers for the gangs, but there was a head driver, too. The head driver, who like all the other drivers was himself a slave, was a person of some importance. When the overseer was away this head driver controlled the drivers and their gangs, decided the work task to be allotted, and administered punishment. In Fanny's words, he exercised

all the functions of undisputed mastery over his fellow slaves, for you will observe that all this occurs while he is as much a slave as any of the rest. Trustworthy, upright, intelligent, he may be flogged tomorrow if Mr. Oden [the overseer] or Mr. Butler so please, and sold the next day, like a cart horse, at the will of the latter.

As soon as Fanny had arrived on Butler Island and settled into the cottage reserved for herself and her family, she lost no time in visiting the plantation infirmary which was located on Number 1, the principal settlement on the island. To get to this building she had to walk down the row of slave huts where the field workers lived. She stopped to inspect these dwellings, and described what she saw:

These cabins consist of one room, about twelve feet by fifteen, with a couple of closets smaller and closer than the staterooms of a ship, divided off from the main room and each other by rough wooden partitions, in which the inhabitants sleep. They have almost all of them a rude bedstead, with the gray moss of the forests for mattress, and filthy, pestilential-looking blankets for

Fanny Kemble's cottage, Butler Island.

covering. Two families (sometimes eight and ten in number) reside in one of these huts, which are mere wooden frames pinned, as it were, to the earth by a brick chimney outside. . . . Attached to each hovel is a small scrap of ground for a garden, which, however, is for the most part untended and uncultivated.

This island plantation produced for its owners an annual income which, in modern currency, might be reckoned, at the very least, at $250,000 a year. But the black people who made this money for their white owners lived in conditions of ultimate wretchedness and poverty. As Fanny observed,

Such of the dwellings as I visited today were filthy and wretched in the extreme, and exhibited the most deplorable consequence of ignorance and an abject condition, the inability of the inhabitants to secure and improve even such pitiful comfort as might yet be achieved by them. . . . Firewood and shavings lay littered about the floors, while the half-naked children were cowering around two or three smouldering cinders. The moss with which the chinks and crannies of their ill-protecting dwellings might have been stuffed was trailing in dirt and dust about the ground, while the back doors of the huts, opening upon a most unsightly ditch, [were] left wide open for fowls and ducks, which they are allowed to raise, to travel in and out, increasing the filth of the cabin by what they brought and left in every direction.

Is Fanny's description an exaggeration? Many Georgia slaves—old-timers who survived the Civil War and told the remembrances of slavery childhood in their old age—have confirmed what she had to tell. Jefferson

Franklin Henry, born in Paulding County, Georgia, in 1859, gave in 1938 this description of his birthplace:

Slave quarters was off from the big house apiece, and they was built in rows like streets. Most of the log cabins had one room; some had two, but all of them had plain old stack chimneys made of sticks and red mud. Our beds was just home-made make-shifts, but us didn't know no difference 'cause us never had seen no better ones. . . . Like them old beds the mattresses us had them days warn't much compared with what we sleeps on now. Them ticks was made of coarse home-wove cloth, called "osnaburg," and them was filled with straw. . . .

Jefferson Henry remembered that the straw in the mattresses "did squeak and cry out when us moved." But in such details as bedding there was much variation from place to place. Butler Island slaves, Fanny noted, slept on "the gray moss of the forests," which may have provided a soft couch for people, but also attracted fleas. Elsewhere field workers, and especially children, made do with a pile of leaves.

Fanny also noted the "pestilential blankets" which slaves were provided with. If they were not warm enough to keep out the cold, one had to sleep in one's clothes. On many big plantations the standard allowance for men was two suits a year made of coarse flannel, which Fanny described as "an extremely stout thick, heavy woolen cloth of a dark gray or blue color." Jefferson Henry described these suits as "jean pants and home-spun shirts," which were warm enough in winter but unbearably uncomfortable during the summer. Boys went barefoot, with a single long shirt that often became so ragged that it hardly covered their nakedness. As Henry described it,

Winter time dey give chillun new cotton and wool mixed shirts what come down most to de ankles. By time hot weather come de shirt was done wore thin and swunk up and 'sides dat us had growed enough for 'em to be short on us, so jus' wore dem same shirts right on thoo' de summer.

Carrie Hudson, born in Elbert County, Georgia, recalled that slave women wore full skirts of the same material as the men, "tathered on to plain, close fittin' waisties. Little gal's dresses was made just like their Ma's." What little money they could make, for example by gathering moss and selling it in the nearby town of Dairien, slave women often spent on "Sunday best." As Fanny Kemble described it, Sunday best included

frills, flounces, ribbons . . . filthy finery, every color in the rainbow, and the deepest possible shades blended in fierce companionship round one dusky visage; head handkerchiefs that put one's eyes out from a mile off; chintzes with sprawling patterns, that might be seen if the clouds were printed with them; beads, bugles, flaring sashes, and, above all, little fanciful aprons, which finish these incongruous toilets with a sort of airy grace.

Her inspection of the huts finished, Fanny came at last to the infirmary. This she described as "a large, two-story building, terminating the broad orange-planted space between the two rows of houses which form the first settlement." It was made of wood, whitewashed, and contained four rooms, two of which, both on the ground floor, were occupied by women. "In the enormous chimney," Fanny wrote,

glimmered the powerless embers of a few sticks of wood, round which, however, as many of the sick women as could approach were cowering, some on wooden settles, most of them on the ground, excluding those who were too ill to rise; and these last poor wretches lay prostrate on the floor, without bed, mattress, or pillow, buried in tattered and filthy blankets which, huddled around them as they lay strewed about, left hardly space to move upon the floor. And here, in their hour of sickness and suffering, lay those whose health and strength are spent in unrequited labor for us—those who, perhaps even yesterday, were being urged on to their unpaid task—those whose husbands, fathers, brothers, and sons were even at that hour sweating over the earth, whose produce was to buy for us all the luxuries which health can revel in, all the comforts which can alleviate sickness.

Gradually Fanny's eyes became accustomed to the dimness of the cold, half-shuttered room.

I stood in the midst of them perfectly unable to speak, the tears pouring from my eyes at this sad spectacle of their misery, myself and my emotion alike strange and incomprehensible to them. Here lay women expecting every hour the terrors and the agonies of childbirth, others who had just brought their doomed offspring into the world, others who were groaning over the anguish and bitter disappointment of miscarriages—here lay some burning with fever, others chilled with cold and aching with rheumatism, upon the hard cold ground, the draughts and the dampness of the atmosphere increasing their sufferings, and dirt, noise and stench, and every aggravation of which sickness is capable, combined in their condition—here they lay like brute beasts. . . .

Was such heartlessness in the treatment of the sick a common feature of American plantations? The Butler estate, like so many others in the South, was the victim of absentee ownership. In other words, the owners had lived for years in their elegant Philadelphia home and had allowed hired managers, or overseers, to run the property and to assume responsibility for it. People like the Butlers judged their overseers by a single criterion: Were they making the property pay? So long as money flowed into the bank, why should the owners worry about the unending sorrows of their slaves? Overseers and managers followed the lead of their employers. Such people, as Fanny noted bitterly, "have nothing to do with sick slaves: they are tools, to be mended only if they can be made available again; if not, to be flung aside as useless, without further expense of money, time, or trouble."

The death rate among the blacks on Butler Island, both adults and young people, was extremely high. Exhausting labor and semi-starvation amid the steamy, fever-ridden swamps took their toll. Said Fanny,

I suppose the general low diet of the Negroes must produce some want of stamina in them; certainly, either from natural constitution or the effect of their habits of existence, or both, it is astonishing how much less power of resistance to disease they seem to possess than we do. If they are ill, the vital energy seems to sink immediately.

Toward the end of January 1839, a young slave named

Shadrach died after an acute illness that lasted only three days. The body was wrapped in a winding sheet of cotton cloth, placed in its pine coffin, and taken to the cottage of "a cooper of the name of London, the head of the religious party of the inhabitants of the island, a Methodist preacher of no small intelligence and influence among the people, who was to perform the religious service." It was late evening, and the day's work was over. There the black people gathered, with Fanny and her husband Pierce among them. The scene was lit by the flaming pine torches that some of the men carried. "Presently," wrote Fanny, "the whole congregation uplifted their voices in a hymn, the first high wailing notes of which, sung all in unison in the midst of these unwonted surroundings—sent a thrill through my nerves."

Here is the song that the people sang:

Lay This Body Down

O grave - yard, ___ O grave - yard, ___ I'm walk - ing through the grave - yard, ___ Lay this bod - y down.

I know starlight,
I'm walking through the starlight,
Lay this body down.

I know moonlight,
I'm walking through the moonlight,
Lay this body down.

I lie in the grave,
I'm lying in the graveyard,
Lay this body down.

O graveyard, O graveyard,
I'm walking through the graveyard,
Lay this body down.

I go to judgment,
In the evening of the day,
Lay this body down.

Your soul and my soul,
Will meet on that day,
Lay this body down.

Graveyard, O graveyard,
I'm walking through the graveyard,
Lay this body down.

Then Reverend London began to speak, and ended by asking God's blessings upon the master, the mistress, and their children. "This," Fanny tells us, "fairly overcame my composure, and I began to cry very bitterly." The throng then moved off to the people's burial ground, which lay between Settlements 3 and 4, with a small clump of trees to one side. The minister began to read the burial service, and as he read Fanny wrestled with her feelings,

the mingled emotions of awe and pity, and an indescribable sensation of wonder at finding myself on this slave soil, surrounded by my slaves, among whom again I knelt *while the words proclaiming to the living and the dead the everlasting covenant of freedom, I am the resurrection and the life, sounded over the prostrate throng and mingled with the heavy flowing of the vast river sweeping not far from where we stood.*

Then the body was lowered into its waterlogged grave, "for the whole island is a mere swamp, off which the Altamaha is only kept from sweeping by the high dikes all around it." At this awful moment the calm of the funeral throng was shattered; frantic exclamations of grief broke out. Fanny, sobbing bitterly, walked home with Pierce along the broad dike. The torchbearers dispersed; and says she, "we found the shining of the stars in the deep blue lovely night sky quite sufficient to light our way."

As Fanny and Pierce walked in silence through the night, they were followed at a distance by a barefoot girl muttering to herself, "a poor gibbering half-witted creature whose mental incapacity, of course, in no respect unfits her for the life of toil, little more intellectual than that of any beast of burden, which is her allotted portion here."

When Major Pierce Butler rose from his labors in writing the American Constitution, he moved southward, to Georgia, to find new lands upon which to plant his slaves. But in those same days when Butler was building his Sea Island fortune, the majority of planters were moving to new fields that lay inland, to the west and southwest. How this happened and what it meant for the Republic and all of its people will take up the rest of our pages.

NEW-FALLEN SNOW
The Cotton Kingdom, 1800–1860

There are few sights more pleasant to the eye than a wide cotton field when it is in bloom. It presents an appearance of purity, like an immaculate expanse of light, new-fallen snow.

Solomon Northup, *Twelve Years a Slave*

The Revolutionary War won for the American Republic a huge stretch of wilderness lying between the Appalachian Mountains and the Mississippi. Roughly one-half of this land lay south of the Ohio River. After 1800 it began to be cleared and planted by settlers fleeing the exhausted lands of the eastern coast. Since Congress had set no limits to the expansion of slavery south of the Ohio, many settlers brought their slaves with them.

Two factors accelerated the movement into this area —that has been labeled the Old Southwest—and, indeed, converted it into a mad rush.

The first factor was the War of 1812 which broke the power of the native American peoples in these lands— primarily the Cherokees, Choctaws, Chikasaws, Seminoles, and Creeks. When the war ended in 1814, pioneers

Ginning cotton.

were free to move in rapidly without having to face and overcome the organized opposition of the original owners of the soil.

The second factor in the land rush that developed after 1800 was the invention of the cotton gin. One of the main attractions for Pierce Butler when he moved to the Sea Islands was the possibility of growing Sea Island cotton—the beautiful, silky, black-seed cotton so much in demand in the textile centers of Great Britain. But Sea Island production was necessarily limited and quite inadequate to meet the booming demand for American cotton. *Gossipium barbadense,* to give it its scientific name, could not be grown away from the humid, semitropical coast. Inland, the climatic conditions simply were not right. A different variety of cotton, green-seed cotton, *could* be grown inland. But there was a problem with this green-seed cotton (called by the botanists *gossipium hirsutum*); it was very hard to separate the lint from the seed, to *gin* it, as the process was called.

This obstacle to the use of green-seed cotton was overcome in 1793, when Eli Whitney invented a new kind of cotton gin. Whitney's invention meant that cotton could now be produced all through the boundless lands of the Southwest where *gossipium hirsutum* could easily be grown because it was adapted to the climatic conditions prevailing there.

Thus, one of the great land rushes of modern history got underway. The revolution that the War of 1812 and the invention of Whitney's gin spelled out for the southern economy is clearly illustrated in the graph on page 27.

As we see, from 1815 until 1859 cotton production was doubling approximately every ten years. Total production in those years rose from 209,000 to 4,500,000 bales. This was surely an astronomical increase. In this period "cotton became king," cotton became the South's dominant crop. Whoever possessed fertile land and slaves to clear and cultivate it could command a fortune.

In the years 1793 to 1814 the Cotton Kingdom began to develop fairly slowly. After that a swift expansion took place, and at an ever accelerating rate. It spread across Georgia into Mississippi and Alabama, which became states in 1817 and 1819 respectively; it rolled across the Mississippi into Missouri and Arkansas, which became states in 1821 and 1836; after the war with Mexico, 1846–1848, it moved onward into the rich coastal lands of Texas. By the Civil War, the Cotton Kingdom, and with it slavery's empire, stretched from the Atlantic Ocean on the east to the Rio Grande on the west, from the Ohio River on the north to the Gulf of Mexico on the south. This was 40 percent of all U.S. land and included 15 of the 32 states that by 1860 made up the Union. Twelve million people lived in this empire, and 4 million of them were black chattels.

How was this great empire cleared so rapidly and made productive so soon? Much of the first settlement and clearing was undertaken by white pioneers moving westward from Virginia, the Carolinas, and Georgia. George Buckingham, noted British traveler, witnessed the painful process in 1840 in Alabama, and described it in his *Slave States of America* published in 1842:

It is difficult for any one living in England to appreciate the difficulties, toils, and privations which a settler

Cotton Production
1795-1860
(000 bales)

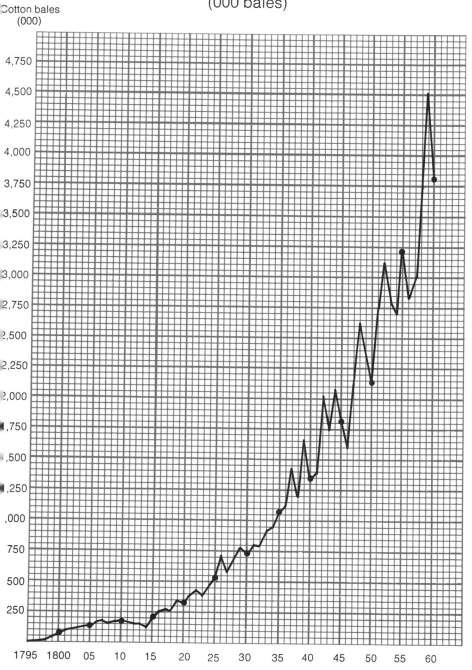

Cotton bales
(000)

YEARS

and his family have to undergo in clearing land, and surrounding themselves with even the barest necessities. Every member of the family must work hard, from daylight to dark, the women as well as the men, and the children as well as the grown people. We saw many boys and girls, of not more than six or seven years of age, some using small axes, others carrying wood, and others assisting in domestic duties. In general they were very dirty in their persons, the mother being too weary to wash them; ragged and ill-fitted in their clothes, there being no tailor or dressmaker to make them. . . . They were all apparently unhealthy, parents and children looking pale and haggard, overworked in body, and over-pressed with thought and anxiety in mind.

The vast majority of these westward-moving whites were too poor to own slaves, though some did indeed possess a slave or two. But hard upon the heels of these first settlers came wealthier people with whole flocks of slaves. As land values and taxes rose, the poorer farmers could not compete with the wealthier and were forced, inexorably, to leave the fertile bottom lands upon which they might have settled. Often these poor white farmers, who had cleared the land at such a sacrifice, were obliged to retreat to the hills—in eastern Kentucky and Tennessee, western Georgia and northern Alabama—to vegetate in poverty and, too often, in squalor. They, as much as the blacks, were victims of a system that dispossessed them and deprived them of their lands.

There were, of course, gradations of wealth and prosperity among the millions of small white farmers. It was the misery of the poor white trash, or pinelanders, at the very bottom of the white social scale, that struck Fanny

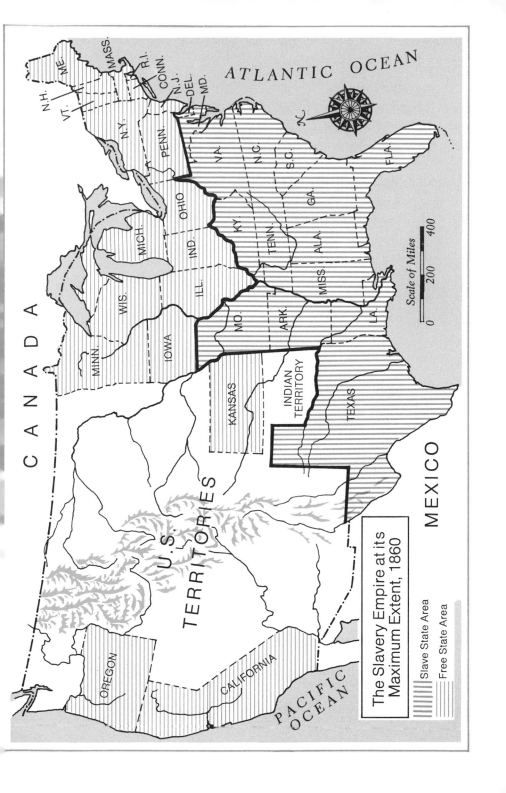

The Slavery Empire at its Maximum Extent, 1860

Slave State Area

Free State Area

Scale of Miles

0   200   400

Kemble when she visited Georgia. She wrote of a visit to the pine barrens:

We passed occasionally a tattered man or woman whose yellow mud complexion, straight features, and singularly sinister countenance bespoke an entirely different race from the Negro population in the midst of which they lived. These are the so-called pinelanders of Georgia, I suppose the most degraded race of human beings claiming an Anglo-Saxon origin that can be found on the face of the earth—filthy, lazy, brutal, ignorant, proud, penniless savages, without one of the nobler attributes which have been found occasionally allied to the vices of savage nature. They own no slaves, for they are almost without exception abjectly poor; they will not work, for that, as they conceive, would reduce them to an equality with the abhorred Negroes; they squat, and steal, and starve, on the outskirts of this lowest of all civilized societies, and their countenances bear witness to the squalor of their condition and the utter degradation of their natures. To the crime of slavery, though they have no profitable part or lot in it, they are fiercely accessory, because it is the barrier that divides the black and white races, at the foot of which they lie wallowing in unspeakable degradation, but immensely proud of the base freedom which still separates them from the lash-driven tillers of the soil.

At the opposite end of the white social scale was the small class of wealthy farmers and planters who dominated the South until the Civil War. Many people have the impression that these farmers and planters lived a life of luxury in mansions with pillars, porticoes, and chandeliers, and with swarms of black servants to feed and fan them. Weary travelers, it has been thought, had only to knock at the doors of these elegant houses to be taken in and entertained with a hospitality that was both bountiful and gracious. All this, it seems, is part of a beautiful southern tradition that has gone with the wind.

Much of it is pure myth. There may have been establishments of this type in old Virginia; Charleston, South Carolina; or New Orleans. Pierce Butler and other coastal planters established princely homes on the Sea Islands. But the majority of planters in the Cotton Kingdom as it spread westward were hard, driving, self-made men who lived under rough conditions; and, if by any chance they agreed to take in a traveler overnight, they charged a dollar or two for the service, which was usually abominable.

Frederick Law Olmsted, the famous writer and conservationist who toured thousands of miles throughout the South from 1852 to 1854, described one such typical planter and his home in Tennessee. Olmsted came, one evening, to

the best house that I had seen during the day, a large, neat, white house, with negro shanties, and an open log cabin in the front yard. A stout, elderly, fine-looking woman, in a cool white muslin dress sat upon the gallery, fanning herself. Two little negroes had just brought a pail of fresh water, and she was drinking of it with a gourd, as I came to the gate. I asked if it would be convenient for her to accommodate me for the night— doubtingly, for I had learned to distrust the accommodations of the wealthy slaveholders.

The woman said yes, and the two of them went into the parlor which, Olmsted noted, "had a bed in it." After a while the planter himself came in, dressed, for the weather was very warm, "merely in a pair of short-legged, unbleached cotton trousers, and a shirt with the bosom open—no shoes or stockings." Supper was then prepared by the two daughters of the house with the assistance of the two little black boys who, earlier, had brought the mistress her pail of fresh water:

The cabin in front of the house was the kitchen, and when the bacon was dished up, one of the boys struck an iron triangle at the door. "Come to supper," said the host, and led the way to the kitchen, which was also the supper room. One of the young ladies took the foot of the table, the other seated herself apart by the fire, and actually waited on the table. . . .

In the course of the supper-table conversation the master of the house told Olmsted that most of the folks around went barefoot all winter, even though there was snow much of the time; nobody wore coats, except on holidays. "That is the healthiest way," the master told Olmsted, "just to toughen yourself, and not wear no coat; no matter how cold it is, I don't wear no coat."

Soon it was bedtime, and Olmsted was taken upstairs to a large room, where he undressed while the master held the candle. Olmsted shared the room with one of the planter's sons; his mattress was of straw, covered with a single sheet. In the morning, when he went downstairs again, he

saw the master lying on his bed in the "parlor," still asleep in the clothes he wore at supper. His wife was

Slaves shipped south from Washington, D.C.

washing herself on the gallery, being already dressed for the day; after drying her face on the family towel, she went into the kitchen, but soon returned, smoking a pipe, to her chair in the doorway.

Everything about this home, Olmsted stressed, "betokened an opulent and prosperous farmer—rich land, extensive field crops, a number of negroes and considerable herds of cattle and horses. He also had capital invested in mines and railroads, he told me. His elder son spoke of him as 'the squire.' "

The westward movement of slavery and the development of the Cotton Kingdom divided the South, very roughly, into two principal zones: the Old South, rich in slaves; and the new, or Deep South, rich in fertile land but suffering from a chronic shortage of black labor to do the work and produce the wealth. In this situation slave owners began to emigrate to the Southwest or to sell off their surplus slaves to plantations in that region. By 1820, slaves had become a valuable cash crop and could be sold at ever-advancing prices to cultivators in the Deep South. Here is how Elige Davison, who was raised in Richmond, Virginia, remembered it:

I been marry once 'fore freedom, with home weddin'. Massa, he bring some more women to see me. He wouldn't let me have jus' one woman. I have 'bout fifteen, and I don't know how many chillen. Some over a hundred, I's sho'.

James Green, another slave, was raised in Petersburg,

Virginia. He said this about his master: "He breeds niggers as quick as he can, 'cause dat money for him. . . . But de nigger husbands wasn't de only ones dat keeps havin' chillen, 'cause de marsters and de drivers takes all de nigger gals dey wants. Den de chillen was brown and I seed one clear white one, but dey slaves jus' de same."

The white planters were growing wealthy supplying the ever-expanding market for cotton. So great was the demand for cotton and for slaves to grow it that the total available supply of American slaves was inadequate to meet it. Until the very end of slavery times, it remained profitable to kidnap black people in Africa and smuggle them into the South in defiance of the law of 1808 banning the international slave traffic. Over and over again this theme recurs in the accounts of slavery given by the slaves themselves: *My grandmammy was seized in Africa, dragged on board ship and brung over here.* Josephine Howard, born in Tuscaloosa, Alabama, about 1848, remembered the searing experience of her mother snatched from Africa when she was a little girl:

Dey always done tell us it am wrong to lie and steal, but why did de white folks steal my mammy and her mammy? Dey lives close to some water, somewheres over in Africy, and de man come in a little boat to de sho' and tell 'em he got presents on de big boat. Most of de men am out huntin' and my mammy and her mammy gits took out to dat big boat and dey locks 'em in a black hole what mammy say so black you can't see nothin'. . . . De captain keep 'em locked in dat black hole till dat boat gits to Mobile and dey is put on de block and sold.

But, the internal slave traffic was more important than the international trade in slaves in the years 1815 to 1860. The business of transferring slaves from the Old South to the New South was in the hands of people called soul-drivers, or speculators. These people bought men, women, and children directly from the plantations, traded them at auctions, gathered them into "lots," and sent them south. William Bost, raised in Newton, North Carolina, told how, when he was about ten years old, in 1858, he saw soul-drivers driving slaves to auction to sell them:

They [the soul drivers] always come 'long on the last of December so that the niggers would be ready for sale on the first day of January. Many the time I see four or five of them chained together. They never had enough clothes to keep a cat warm. The women never wore anything but a thin dress and a petticoat and one underwear. I've seen the ice balls hangin' on to the bottom of their dresses as they ran along like sheep in a pasture before they are sheared. They never wore any shoes. Just run along on the ground all spewed up with ice.

Thus it came about that black slaves crowded the river steamers that plied the Ohio and the Mississippi, or crowded the coastal vessels that plied to Mobile and New Orleans, or wound in weary coffles across the overland trails.

Many writers have described these travels. In 1846, for example, William Seward, well-known New York lawyer who had served as governor of the state, was taking ship at Norfolk, Virginia. He saw a gang of slaves

Slave auction, Richmond, Virginia.

shipped from there and bound for New Orleans. Seventy-five slaves were led on board, all young, some still children, each carrying a bundle or box containing all that he or she had in the world. When the slaver sailed, it carried a total of two hundred slaves. "The captain of our boat," said Seward,

seeing me intensely interested, turned to me and said: "Oh, sir, do not be concerned about them; they are the happiest people in the world!" I looked, and there they were—slaves, ill protected from the cold, fed capriciously on the commonest food—going from all that was dear to all that was terrible, and still they wept not.

Not only traders, but to an even greater extent ordinary farmers and big plantation owners, drove slaves on the overland routes to the Deep South. One such farmer, headed for the South and a cotton fortune, was described by James K. Paulding, then secretary of the navy, during an excursion in 1816 to Virginia:

The sun was shining out very hot—and in turning the angle of the road, we encountered the following group: first, a little cart drawn by one horse, in which five or six half-naked black children were tumbled like pigs together. The cart had no covering, and they seemed to have been broiled to sleep. Behind the cart marched three black women, with head, neck, and breasts uncovered, and without shoes or stockings: next came three men, bareheaded and chained together with an ox-chain. Last of all, came a white man on horseback, carrying his pistols in his belt. . . .

James Buckingham, the British traveler whom we met earlier in this chapter, encountered a much larger slave drove near Fredericksburg, Virginia, in 1839. He wrote:

The weather was so excessively cold as to require all the cloaks we could wrap around us, and to have the curtains and the windows of the coach closed at the same time. . . . Two miles beyond Fredericksburg . . . we met a gang of slaves, including men, women, and children, the men chained together in pairs, and the women carrying the children and bundles, in their march to the South. The gang was under several white drivers, who rode near them on horseback, with large whips, while the slaves marched on foot beside them; and there was one driver behind, to bring up the rear.

Buckingham pointed out that the slave men were chained together to prevent violence against their white tormentors, and to prevent escape. "When accompanied by one or two white men . . . they might be tempted to rise against them in any solitary part of the road, or, at the least, to escape from them if they could; both of which, this chaining them together renders impossible."

When the black people arrived at their destination, some of them were sold at auction. Some became cooks, craftsmen, body servants. The fate of the majority was to toil in the cotton, sugar, and tobacco fields from dawn to dusk, more than three hundred days a year, until they could toil no more. Day after day, year after year, as the sun rose over the Atlantic its first rays summoned millions of these black toilers to their daily labor; and when, many hours later, it sank redly into the Pacific, these same toilers were still at their toil.

The slave empire, until 1860, was almost entirely rural, for there were few factories in the South, few railroad lines, few big towns. Most slaves worked in the fields, and most worked, not on small farms owned by small farmers, but on the huge tracts owned by a tiny group of slaveholders. By 1860 there were 4 million black slaves in the South, and 8 million free white people. Of these whites, only about half a million owned any slaves at all. The majority of the black people were owned by, and worked for, 10,000 wealthy planters. This tiny class, affluent and immensely powerful, ruled the South until the end of the Civil War. It made the law, molded morals and beliefs, controlled the destinies of all the people in the vast southern land.

Men and women alike toiled in the fields, but with a

difference, because the women suffered a double oppression. Like the men they were obliged to labor, to produce wealth for their masters; and they were also obliged to produce the workers of the next generation. The children, black, brown, and white, that they conceived, bore, and gave birth to, were not their own, to cherish, raise, and educate as they wished. If the mother was a slave, the child was a slave too. That's what *slave* meant: to be owned body and soul by another, by a white person (usually a man); to have no control over yourself, your life, your future; to be bound, totally, from birth to death. Children might be torn from their mothers and sold; and the mothers might be torn from their lovers and their children, and sold.

Women who were with child had to work, for were they not workers, and should they not be beaten if they were lazy? Ann Clark, who was born in 1825 in Mississippi, worked hard all her life. "I ploughed, hoed, split rails. I done the hardest work ever a man ever did." And here is her judgment upon slavery: "When women was with child they'd dig a hole in the groun' and put their stomach in the hole, and then beat 'em."

The double role and the double pain of women was told by Elvira Boles, also born in Mississippi, the slave of Elihu Boles of Lexington who ran a brickyard as well as a farm. "Marster Boles," said she,

didn't have many slaves on de farm, but lots in de brickyard. I toted brick back and put 'em down where dey had to be. Six bricks each load all day. That's de reason I ain't no 'count, I'se worked to death. I fired de furnace for three years. Standin' front wid de hot fire on my face. Hard work, but God was wid me. We'd work til dark, quit awhile after sundown. Marster was good to slaves, didn't believe in jus' lashin' 'em. He'd not be brutal but he'd kill 'em dead right on the spot. . . . I'se seventeen, maybe, when I married to slave of Boles. Married on Saturday night. Dey give me a dress and dey had things to eat, let me have something like what you call a party. . . . And then I had to work every day. I'd leave my baby cryin' in de yard and he'd be cryin', but I couldn't stay. Done everything but split rails. I've cut timber and ploughed. Done everything a man could do. I couldn't notice de time, but I'd be glad to git back to my baby.

Cotton, we have said, was the most important of the southern crops. British and American manufacturers, merchants and growers all grew rich from this industry. The foundation of their wealth was the unpaid labor that black people were driven to year-round under the lash.

Growing cotton was hard work, and it took all year. In January and February the land must be plowed to prepare it for the seed. Oxen and mules were used, both men and women driving the teams and caring for the animals. This required endurance and skill. Bill Homer, born in 1850, recalled plowing for his owner in Caldwell, Texas:

You never drive de ox, did you? De mule ain't stubborn side of de ox, de ox am stubborn, and den some more. One time I'se haulin' fence rails and de oxen starts to turn go when I wants dem to go ahead. I calls for haw, but dey pays dis nigger no mind and keeps agwine go. Den day starts to run and de overseer hollers and asks me "Whar you gwine?" I hollers back "I's not gwine, I's bein' took."Dem oxen takes me to de well for water, 'cause if dey gits dry and is near water, dey goes in spite of de devil.

After the plowing was done, seeding took place. A plow was drawn along the ridges between the furrows, and a boy or girl followed behind with a bag of seed. In back of the sower, again, was another mule-drawn plow to cover up the seed.

The seeding operation might consume two months, March and April. In a matter of days the cotton would spring up and hoeing would begin—"scraping cotton," as the black people called it, or chopping away the grass and weeds from around the growing plants. And as soon as a field was hoed, the weeds would spring up again, and the work would have to be done over.

The endless, wearisome operation of cotton scraping would take up another two months until about the middle of July. The slave gangs would be seen advancing in lines across the fields with their eyes fixed to the ground, repeating over and over the same wooden, plodding motion. Solomon Northup, a free man who was kidnaped and enslaved in 1842 and sent to work in Louisiana, described the scene:

The fastest hoer takes the lead row. He is usually about a rod in advance of his companions. If one of them passes him he is whipped. If one falls behind or is a moment idle, he is whipped. In fact, the lash is flying from morning until night, the whole day long. The hoeing season thus continues from April until July, a field having no sooner been finished once, than it is commenced again.

Harvesting cotton.

By late August the crop was ripe for harvest, each field a sea of white where the bolls had split and the fluffy fibers showed. "There are few sights," wrote Northup, "more pleasant to the eye, than a wide cotton field when it is in bloom. It presents an appearance of purity, like an immaculate expanse of light, new-fallen snow."

Again the slave gangs must go through the fields, walking down the furrows row by row, each worker armed with a gunny sack and his own large basket at the end of the row. Daily quotas were assigned to each individual, and these quotas varied from person to person in accordance with his or her skill. Northup explained how these quotas were assigned:

When a new hand, one unaccustomed to the business, is sent into the field, he is whipped up smartly, and made for that day to pick as fast as he can possibly. At night it is weighed, so that his capability in cotton picking is known. He must bring in the same weight each night following. If it falls short, it is considered evidence that he has been laggard, and a greater or less number of lashes is the penalty.

Each day, during the harvest season, the pickers must pick up their baskets after sundown and take them to the overseer to be weighed. Each day human beings were weighed in the overseer's scales and justice was done amid the sound of curses, screams, and sobs. Northup described the torments that the bone-weary pickers experienced during the harvest season when the sun set:

The day's work over in the field, the baskets are

"toted," or in other words, carried to the gin-house, where the cotton is weighed. No matter how fatigued and weary he may be—no matter how much he longs for sleep and rest—a slave never approaches the gin-house with his basket of cotton but with fear. If it falls short in weight—if he has not performed the full task appointed him, he knows that he must suffer. And if he has exceeded it by ten or twenty pounds, in all probability his master will measure the next day's task accordingly. So, whether he has too little or too much, his approach to the gin-house is always with fear and trembling. . . . After weighing follow the whippings; and then the baskets are carried to the cotton house, and their contents stored away like hay, all hands being sent in to tramp it down.

Then the chores had to be done—animals had to be watered and fed, wood had to be cut. The slaves, almost too stiff and tired to stand, were permitted finally to go to their huts, where the children they had not seen all day were already asleep. No one had eaten since a hasty lunch break, many hours before. Now corn must be ground and supper prepared. For most field hands the weekly allowance was a peck of corn, three to four pounds of bacon, a pint of salt. Corn ground and baked, bacon broiled, it was time for supper. In the harvest season this might not be until midnight.

Hardly had the slaves fallen asleep when, one hour before dawn, the overseer's horn was heard. And again the slaves must get up, snatch breakfast, prepare lunch, and hasten to the field while their children were still sleeping.

After the cotton crop had been brought in, the corn

had to be harvested. It was grown for the double purpose of fattening hogs and feeding slaves, and raising it absorbed much of the time that slaves were not employed in the cotton fields. As Northup described it,

It is the white variety, the ear of great size, and the stalk growing to the height of eight, and oftentimes ten feet. In August the leaves are stripped off, dried in the sun, bound in small bundles, and stored away as provender for the mules and oxen. . . . Then the ears are separated from the stalks and deposited in the corncrib with the husks on. . . . Ploughing, planting, picking cotton, gathering corn, and pulling and burning stalks, occupies the whole of the four seasons of the year.

Such, year after year, was the outward scene on the broad fields where slaves toiled all across the southland. How did black people feel about the existence they were compelled to lead? How did they feel about the theft of their lives and their labor, and what did they do about it?

Hushabye

Hushabye,
Don't you cry,
Go to sleepy, little baby;
Way down yonder,
In the meadow,
There's a poor little lambie,
The bees and the butterflies
Pickin' out his eyes,
The poor little thing cries "Mammy!"
Hushabye,
Don't you cry,
Go to sleepy, little baby.

DOWN IN THE WILDERNESS
The Daily Struggle, 1800–1860

I sought my Lord down in-a wilderness,
In-a wilderness
In-a wilderness
I sought my Lord down in-a wilderness,
For I'm a-goin' home.

Slave song

The black people of the South waged their own struggle against the slave empire with little outside support. For many years Americans have refused to recognize the existence of this struggle, and have been blind to the extraordinary nature of its reality. When William Seward, as was described in the last chapter, witnessed black people being sold into exile, the captain's answer was, *don't worry, they're happy.* Seward found it hard to believe this —evidence to the contrary, after all, was staring him in the face. But millions of Americans, since that time, have swallowed the comforting myth that slaves were happy. It is hard to face the fact that your people, your government, your country, have committed an abominable crime. A lot of people have looked for an out, and there has been no scarcity of historians who have asserted loudly that black people were content with slavery, and who have tried to prove it. Novels, history texts, and movies all have given a picture of cheerful, banjo-plucking darkies happy as larks under the supervision of wise and humane white people.

The noted historian Ulrich B. Phillips played an important part in fashioning this racist myth. Slavery in the South, Phillips asserted, was a civilization with a self-imposed mission to educate and humanize "black savages." If Phillips is to be believed, the best thing that the United States ever did was to grab millions of black people and bring them to these shores. This, in his view, was a "rescue operation" that saved the poor people from the darkness of African superstition and exposed them to the kindly and uplifting influences of that best of all schools for blacks, the southern plantation.

Black people, in Phillips' view, were content with this situation; like the captain said, they loved it, and did not rebel except in rare instances. Why should they? Plantations, Phillips said, "were the best school yet invented for the mass training of that sort of inert and backward people which the American negroes represented." This training Phillips labeled "benign": the slaves received medical care when sick, food and clothing, healthy out-of-doors work, and fun—security, in fact, from the cradle to the grave. "The bulk of the slaves," as he wrote, "because they were negroes, because they were costly, and because they were in personal touch, were pupils and working wards, while the planters were teachers and guardians as well as owners."

Phillips wrote a number of books to prove his thesis. Even if we are impressed by his claims to scholarship, we have every reason to be dubious about his view of human nature. The fact is, if people are deeply wronged they will try, as best they can, to do something about it. Shakespeare eloquently expressed this truth in *The Merchant of Venice*. Shylock, the Jewish merchant, is asked why he seeks revenge against Antonio, who has wronged him. "I am a Jew," he answers,

I am a Jew. Hath not a Jew eyes? Hath not a Jew hands, organs, dimensions, senses, affections, passions? Fed with the same food, hurt with the same weapons, subject to the same diseases, healed by the same means, warmed and cooled by the same winter and summer, as a Christian is? If you prick us, do we not bleed? If you tickle us, do we not laugh? If you poison us, do we not die? And if you wrong us, shall we not revenge?

When people are wronged we must look for evidence of anger, resistance, and a struggle for revenge—a struggle to reassert your humanity against the violence of those who would rob you of it. Slaveholders, of course, taught their slaves that they should not offer resistance to evil; they urged them to accept their lot in this world, and promised that God would assuredly reward them in Heaven. Slaves may have found some merit in this advice, but they did not follow it consistently. Harriet Beecher Stowe, in a book on slavery that she entitled *A Key to Uncle Tom's Cabin,* explained why. She pointed out that slavery must of necessity be a terribly harsh form of rule because it had to control and to contain the most explosive force in the world, the fury of the human soul. "When we consider," she wrote,

that the material thus to be acted upon is that fearfully explosive element, the soul of man; that soul elastic, up-

springing, immortal, whose free will even the omnipotence of God refuses to coerce,—we may form some idea of the tremendous force which is necessary to keep this mightiest of elements in the state of repression which is contemplated in the definition of slavery.

Slaves lived in perpetual fear—fear of producing too little, fear of oversleeping, fear of the searing, bloody lash that cowed them into outward submission. But we must also look at the other side of the coin: the slaveholders, too, lived in perpetual terror of the black volcano upon which they sat. The violence they used was an exact expression of their understanding that human beings could not be kept in slavery without the constant threat of brutal punishment if they dared to resist or to rebel.

Open, armed rebellion by slaves against their masters took place only at fairly infrequent intervals. But this does not mean that there was not a daily struggle against slavery which took many different forms—as many forms as the ingenuity of a slave could find or invent. Fanny Kemble, with rare perception, went to the heart of the matter when she wrote about Butler Island: *"There is the most disgusting struggle which is going on the whole time, on the one hand to inflict, and on the other to evade oppression and injustice."*

One form of resistance was simply to hide during work hours and count on not being missed. Frederick Law Olmsted described a situation that he witnessed personally on a large cotton plantation in northern Alabama in 1857. The plantation overseer, in riding his horse across a deep brush-covered gully, flushed out a young black woman, about eighteen years of age. She had an explanation of her presence there, but the overseer did not bother to check it out. "That won't do," he said, "get down." "The girl," continued Olmsted,

knelt on the ground; he got off his horse, and holding her with his left hand, struck her thirty or forty blows across the shoulders with his tough, flexible, raw-hide whip. . . . At every stroke the girl winced and exclaimed "Yes, sir!" or "Ah, sir!" or "Please, sir!" not groaning or screaming. The girl repeated the same story. "You have not got enough yet," said he; "pull up your clothes—lie down." The girl without any hesitation, without a word or look of remonstrance or entreaty, drew closely all her garments under her shoulders, and lay down upon the ground with her face toward the overseer, who continued to flog her with the raw-hide. . . . She now shrunk away from him, not rising, but writhing, grovelling, and screaming, "Oh, don't sir! oh please stop, master! please sir! oh, that's enough, master! oh, Lord! oh, master, master! oh, God, master, do stop! oh, God, master! oh God, master!"

As the men rode away they were followed by the sound of choking, spasmodic sobs. Never before had Olmsted seen a woman flogged. *Was it necessary,* he asked the overseer, as soon as he could trust himself to speak, *to punish her so severely?* "Oh, yes, sir," the overseer replied, "if I hadn't, she would have done the same thing tomorrow, and half the people on the plantation would have followed her example."

The overseer's inhuman punishment, then, was not directed simply at one black woman, but at *all* the people on the plantation. Even a single instance of hiding from work presented a challenge to his control. To overcome that challenge he must make it clear to everybody what the consequences of even the slightest resistance to his rule would be.

On other occasions, slaves defied their masters when threatened with punishment and refused to allow themselves to be beaten. Such defiance resulted in terrifying punishment because the master saw in it an act of resistance that might flame into mass revolt and thus put an end to slavery itself. Frederick Douglass, famous black leader who escaped from slavery in Maryland in 1838, told about just such an incident in the classic *Narrative of the Life of Frederick Douglass* that he published in 1845. Austin Gore was the overseer of the plantation upon which Douglass was working; one day Gore began to whip a slave named Demby, but Demby refused to take it. He plunged into a creek and stood in the middle of the stream with the water up to his neck, and refused to move. Three times Gore called to him to come out of the water, but Demby did not budge. The overseer then raised his gun to his shoulder and blew the defiant slave out of existence. This act of cold-blooded murder he defended in the following words:

Demby had become unmanageable. He was setting a dangerous example to the other slaves, one which, if suffered without some such demonstration on his part, would finally lead to the total subversion of all rule and order upon the plantation. . . . If one slave refused to be corrected, and escapes with his life, the other slaves will soon copy the example; the result of which will be, the freedom of the slaves, and the enslavement of the whites.

Gore shooting Denby.

Gore's argument made sense to his employer, Colonel Lloyd. There was no investigation of the murder of Demby, and there was no trial. Gore continued to live and work in Talbot County as a respected member of the community.

A slave who successfully defied his master or overseer was, in spirit at least, no longer a slave. Douglass himself beat a planter named Covey for whom he worked, and who treated him unmercifully. It was, as he recalled,

the turning point in my career as a slave. It rekindled the few expiring embers of freedom, and revived within me a sense of my own manhood. It recalled the departed self-confidence, and inspired me again with a determination to be free. . . . My long-crushed spirit rose, cowardice departed, bold defiance took its place; and I now resolved that, however long I might remain a slave in form, the day had passed forever when I could be a slave in fact. I did not hesitate to let it be known of me, that the white man who expected to succeed in whipping must also succeed in killing me.

Thus slaves who committed acts of protest or vengeance reasserted their manhood or womanhood in the face of a system that would reduce them to the level of faceless brutes, and proclaimed a revolutionary slogan: Liberty or Death. Such endless acts of individual sabotage and revenge occurred throughout the slave empire; plows were broken, houses and barns burned, food poisoned, masters or overseers murdered. Solomon Northup recorded one such act of heroic resistance, and its tragic end. "The gallows were standing at Marksville last January," he wrote, upon which a slave was executed a year ago for killing his overseer. . . . The slave was given his task at splitting rails. In the course of the day the overseer sent him on an errand, which occupied so much time that it was not possible for him to perform his task. The next day he was called to an account, but the loss of time occasioned by the errand was no excuse, and he was ordered to kneel and bare his back for the reception of the lash. They were in the woods alone—beyond the reach of sight and hearing. The boy submitted until maddened at such injustice, and insane with pain, he sprang to his feet, and seizing an axe, literally chopped the overseer to pieces. . . . He was led to the scaffold, and while the rope was round his neck, maintained an undismayed and fearless bearing, and with his last words justified the act.

Yet another form of protest was self-mutilation or suicide. Here is the story that Delicia Patterson, born in Missouri in 1845, told about what happened when she was put up for sale while still a girl:

When I was fifteen years old, I was brought to the courthouse, put up on the auction block to be sold. Old Judge Miller from my county was there. I knew him well because he was one of the wealthiest slave owners in the county, and the meanest one. He was so cruel all the slaves and many owners hated him because of it. He saw me on the block for sale, and he knew I was a good worker. So, when he bid for me, I spoke right out on the auction block and told him: "Old Judge Miller, don't you bid for me, 'cause if you do, I would not live on your plantation. I will take a knife and cut my own throat from ear to ear before I would be owned by you."

A black suicide, 1817.

One very common form of protest was to flee to the woods, swamps, or caves and hide out. Slaves stayed in these hideouts for days, weeks, even years, but usually the period was short—the people were forced back by cold or hunger. Some masters regarded such flights as a kind of safety valve, but most of them punished the fugitives with flogging upon their return. Many lost their lives through such flight—as the result of cold, snakebite, exposure, or hunger. Jacob Branch, of Double Bayou, Texas, born in 1851, told of how a slave called Charlie ran off because he was unable to finish a task before the return of his master and wished to escape the promised lashing:

Massa go on de trip and he tell Charlie iffen he ain't finish grinding all de corn meal by Monday he gwineter give him a thousand lashes. He try, but he ain't able to make dat much meal, so come Monday he runned off to de Bayou. Dat night come de big freeze and he down dere with water up to de knees and when massa come home and go git him, he so froze he couldn't walk. Dey bring him in de kitchen and old missy cuss him out. Soon's he thaw out, he done die right dere on de spot.

Julia Brown, born in 1854, pointed out that slaves hiding out could often count upon the help of other slaves in feeding them:

Sometimes the slaves would run away. Their masters was mean to them that caused them to run away. Sometimes they would live in caves. How did they get along? Well, chile, they got along all right—what with other people slippin' things to 'em. And, too, they'd steal hogs, chickens, and anything else they could git their hands on.

Some white people would help, too, for there was some white people who didn't believe in slavery. Yes, they'd try and find them slaves that run away and if they was found they'd be beat or sold to somebody else. My grandmother ran away from her master. She stayed in the woods and she washed her clothes in the branches. She used sand for soap. Yes, chile, I reckon they got along all right in the caves. They had babies in thar, and raised 'em, too.

To the slave owner one runaway challenged the whole system. If all did like one, and were not caught, it would be the end of slavery. So runaways were, in a deep sense, leaders of their people. They had to be brave to run, brave to stay at large, brave to face the tortures that awaited them when caught. Esther Easter, born in 1852 near Memphis, Tennessee, said:

A runaway slave from the Henkin's plantation was brought back and there was a public whipping, so's the slaves could see what happens when they tries to get away. The runaway was chained to the whipping post, and I was full of misery when I see the lash cutting deep into that boy's skin. He swell up like a dead horse, but he gets over it, only he was never no 'count for work no more.

Acts of individual resistance such as these were not as isolated as they might seem but were nourished by a deep sense of black solidarity. This sense was sustained by the common religion which slaves practiced, by their shared rituals and beliefs. With increasing speed toward the end of the eighteenth century, black people in the United States had become converts to Christianity and had

A black funeral.

adopted the same Protestant faith as the majority of the whites. In some places slaves were allowed to attend the white man's church—sitting in the back, or in the gallery; in some places, not. But this made little difference. Slaves all over the South organized their own religious life and held their own secret prayer meetings. They gathered in "big holes," or hollows in the fields or at night in the huts. An iron pot, upended, was placed in the center of the circle. There the people prayed out loud to God, called upon heaven for freedom and deliverance, danced sacred dances, and sang. In such sessions the black believers faced the cruel realities of slavery together, drew strength to face its ordeals from the common bonds which they forged with one another.

Many of the songs, or spirituals, that black people composed were created at these religious sessions, and they played a unique role in the education of whole generations of slaves. Spirituals uttered a complaint, told a story, gave utterance to a vision of the world and of human fate. They bound the people together with a common consciousness of their human dignity and of their common destiny. They gave strength to face the pain of life under slavery when this pain must be accepted, and there was little to be done; and the spirituals also summoned the people to sustained protest against that same fate when the time was right. An insight into how the spirituals were composed is given by Lorenza Ezell, born in Spartanburg, South Carolina, in 1850:

De Baptist Church have a shed built behind de pulpit for cullud folks, with de dirt floor and split log seat for de women folks, but most of de men folks stands or kneels on de floor. Us makes up songs, 'cause us couldn't read or write. . . .

Both in the prayer meetings and in the course of their daily life black people composed their songs and brought into being a new American music that would be recognized, one day, as having worldwide significance. Few white people before the Civil War either understood or appreciated the deep meaning and beauty of what they referred to, contemptuously, as "nigger music." Frederick Douglass, himself a slave, was one of the first to point out the meaning of the spirituals:

They breathed the prayer and complaint of souls boiling over with the bitterest anguish. Every tone was a testimony against slavery, and a prayer to God for deliverance from chains. The hearing of those wild notes always depressed my spirit, and filled me with ineffable sadness. . . . These songs still follow me, to deepen my hatred of slavery, and quicken my sympathies for my brethren in bonds. . . . The songs of the slave represent the sorrows of his heart; and he is relieved by them, only as an aching heart is relieved by its tears.

Poor Rosy

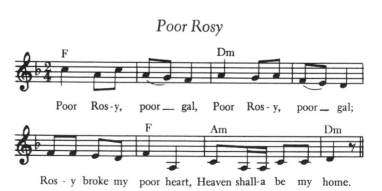

Poor Ros-y, poor __ gal, Poor Ros-y, poor __ gal;

Ros-y broke my poor heart, Heaven shall-a be my home.

Chorus

Be - fore I stay __ in __ hell one day,

Heaven shall-a be my home; I'll __ sing and pray __ my __

soul a - way, Heaven shall-a be my home.

Got hard trials on my way,
Got hard trials on my way,
Got hard trials on my way,
    Heaven shall-a be my home.
O when I walk and talk with God,
    Heaven shall-a be my home.
O when I walk and talk with God,
    Heaven shall-a be my home.

I got troubles on my way,
I got troubles on my way,
I got troubles on my way,
    Heaven shall-a be my home.
Before I stay in hell one day,
    Heaven shall-a be my home.
I'll sing and pray my soul away,
    Heaven shall-a be my home.

Down in the Wilderness 65

River Jordan, I'm bound to go,
River Jordan, I'm bound to go,
River Jordan I am bound to go,
    Heaven shall-a be my home.
Before I stay in hell one day,
    Heaven shall-a be my home.
I'll sing and pray my soul away,
    Heaven shall-a be my home.

Brother Robert, I'm bound to go,
Brother Robert, I'm bound to go,
Brother Robert, I'm bound to go,
    Heaven shall-a be my home.
O when I walk and talk with God,
    Heaven shall-a be my home.
O when I walk and talk with God,
    Heaven shall-a be my home.

Sister Lucy, I'm bound to go,
Sister Lucy, I'm bound to go,
Sister Lucy, I am bound to go,
    Heaven shall-a be my home.
Before I stay in hell one day,
    Heaven shall-a be my home.
I'll sing and pray my soul away,
    Heaven shall-a be my home.

Poor Rosy, poor gal,
Poor Rosy, poor gal,
Rosy stole my poor heart,
    Heaven shall-a be my home.
Oh, when I walk and talk with God,
    Heaven shall-a be my home.
Oh, when I walk and talk with God,
    Heaven shall-a be my home.

The power of religion in the lives of the slaves is illustrated by the story of the prophetess Sinda on Butler Island, who led and organized a general strike of the black workers against their owners. A few years before Fanny Kemble came to the island in 1839, Sinda had let it be known that the world was coming to an end and that it was time to prepare to enter the Kingdom of Heaven. Everybody dropped their tools and refused to work. Wrote Fanny Kemble:

The belief in her assertion took such possession of the people on the estate that they refused to work, and the rice and cotton fields were threatened with an indefinite fallow in consequence of this strike on the part of the cultivators. . . . The great final emancipation which they believed at hand had stripped even the lash of its prevailing authority, and the terrors of an overseer for once were as nothing in the terrible expectation of the advent of the universal Judge of men.

The day that Sinda prophesied as the day of doom came—and went. The prophetess was mercilessly flogged, and the slaves returned to work; faith in the lash replaced faith in Sinda. "Think," concluded Fanny Kemble, "what a dream that must have been while it lasted for those infinitely oppressed people—freedom without entering it by the grim gate of death."

The struggle to believe what you will about the world and life is closely connected with the struggle for literacy. Planters were well aware that reading and writing encouraged communication, ideas, solidarity, dissatisfaction, revolt; all southern states had laws prohibiting the education of black people and punishing those found guilty of carrying on educational work. The Virginia Code of 1819 stated that "any school for teaching them reading or writing, either in the day or the night, under whatsoever pretext, shall be deemed and considered an unlawful assembly." The punishment for those taking part in such meetings was twenty lashes. A delegate to the Virginia House of Delegates said triumphantly in 1832, after more severe laws had been passed:

We have, as far as possible, closed every avenue by which light might enter their minds. If we could extinguish the capacity to see the light, our work would be completed; they would then be on a level with the beasts of the field, and we should be safe!

Elijah Green, a slave born in Charleston, South Carolina, in 1843, put it like this: "For God's sake don't let a slave be cotched with pencil or paper. That was a major crime: you might as well have killed your master or mistress."

For black people, then, the struggle for literacy was central in the struggle against slavery. When Fanny Kemble was about to leave Butler Island and go back north, the slave minister, London, asked her to send him Bibles and prayer books. London, of course, refused to tell her how he organized the reading classes on Butler Island, but it was clear that many Butler Island slaves could indeed read. "Certainly," Fanny concluded, "the science of reading must be more common among the Negroes than I supposed."

Some slaves were taught by their masters or mistresses in defiance of the law. When Frederick Douglass as a child of eight years went to work for Colonel Auld in Maryland, Mrs. Auld began to teach him his letters, but the colonel soon put a stop to that. "If you teach that nigger how to read," he told his wife, "there would be no keeping him. It would forever unfit him to be a slave." The lessons stopped, but Douglass learned to read anyway. He enlisted the help of white kids his own age, made friends with them, gave them bread to eat in return for tuition. Black kids used the same tactics in other parts of the South. Green Cumby, born in Texas in 1851, recalled that "de white chillun learned us to read and write."

Slaves manufactured their own pens and ink, and practiced writing in secret. Gus Feaster, born in South Carolina in 1840, recalled that

Edmund Carlisle, smartest nigger I'se ever seed. He cut out blocks from pine bark on pine tree and smooth it. Git white oak or hickory stick. Git a ink ball from de oak trees, and on Saturday and Sunday slip off where de white folks wouldn't know 'bout it. He use stick fer pen an drap oak ball in water and it be his ink after it done stood all night. He learnt to write his name and how to make figures.

The inevitable climax to the daily struggle against slavery carried on patiently over a period of years was open, organized revolt.

Long Summer Day

Long sum - mer day   make a white man   la - zy,

Long   sum - mer   day.

Long sum - mer day   make a   slave   run a - way   sir,

Final Ending

Long   sum - mer   day.

Long summer day make a white man lazy,
    Long summer day.
Long summer day make a white man lazy,
    Long summer day.

Long summer day make a slave run away sir,
    Long summer day.
Long summer day make a slave run away sir,
    Long summer day.

Pickin' that cotton in the bottom of the field,
    Long summer day.
Yes a-gettin' of the cotton in the bottom of the field sir,
    Long summer day.

Long summer day make a white man lazy,
    Long summer day.
Yes a long summer day make a slave run away sir,
    Long summer day.

Massa and missus sittin' in the parlor,
    Long summer day.
Jes' a figurin' and a studyin' how to make a slave work harder,
    Long summer day.

Well a long summer day make a nigger run away sir,
    Long summer day.
Long summer day make a slave run away sir,
    Long summer day.

Run away to see his Mary,
    Long summer day.
Run away to see his baby,
    Long summer day.

Long summer day make a slave run away sir,
    Long summer day.
Long summer day make a slave run away sir,
    Long summer day.

Collected, adapted and arranged by John A. Lomax & Alan Lomax, TRO © Copyright 1941 and renewed 1968 by Ludlow Music, Inc., New York. Used by permission.

Down in the Wilderness 71

JESUS IS BLACK
Nat Turner, 1831

Then shall the righteous man stand in great boldness before the face of such as have afflicted him, and made no account of his labors. When they see it, they shall be troubled with terrible fear, and shall be amazed at the strangeness of his salvation, so far beyond all they looked for.

The Wisdom of Solomon

Open rebellion, when slaves took matters into their own hands and rose in arms against their oppressors, occurred in scattered places throughout the South from time to time. In 1800, for example, a slave called Gabriel made plans for a revolt in Henrico County, Virginia; in 1822, Denmark Vesey, a free black person, organized an uprising in Charleston, South Carolina. Such rebellions struck panic into the slaveholders' hearts: a single revolt, was it not the spark which might ignite "that fearfully explosive element, the soul of man," so that the whole system would go up in flames?

Greatest of slave rebellions in the heyday of the Cotton Kingdom was Nat Turner's revolt. It began on August 21, 1831, in tidewater Virginia's Southampton County; a company of about seventy slaves rose up and massacred fifty-five whites. In suppressing the revolt hysterical Virginians butchered hundreds of black people, most of whom were innocent of any connection at all with Nat Turner.

Nat Turner himself was captured on October 30, 1831. While he sat in jail at the county seat, Jerusalem, awaiting trial, he gave a full account of the insurrection to a white man, Thomas R. Gray. Gray took down faithfully all that Turner said, and published his story as a pamphlet entitled *The Confessions of Nat Turner*. This pamphlet remains our basic source for the history of the revolt. At his trial Turner refused to plead guilty. He was executed on November 11, 1831.

Nat Turner was born in 1800 in Southampton County, the property of a slave owner named Benjamin Turner. While still a small child he had a sense of his own destiny, that the Lord had chosen and marked him out as a prophet—like Sinda, on Butler Island, a leader of his people. As he told Gray, "My father and mother strengthened me in this my first impression, saying in my presence, I was intended for some great purpose, which they had always thought from certain marks on my head and breast." Turner's grandmother echoed his parents' views. He had, she said, "too much sense to be raised [as a slave], and if I was, I would never be of any service, as a slave."

Nat Turner clearly owed much to his family, above all the knowledge that he was loved, and the deep sense of black identity with which they endowed him. His parents, for example, taught him to read, taught him so young that he had no remembrance in later life of the circumstances under which he learned the alphabet. This love of learning, he tells us, followed him always.

Nat Turner grew up a thoughtful and meditative young man. He was a field worker. As he followed the plow he spoke secretly with God; wild, passionate dreams chased through his mind. More and more he became confirmed in the belief "that I was ordained for some great purpose in the hands of the Almighty."

When the Holy Spirit spoke to Turner, this was the message that he heard: "Seek ye the kingdom of Heaven, and all things shall be added to you." Several years passed as Turner pondered the meaning of this. He became more and more deeply convinced that he must prepare himself to take action, to carry out the divine will.

In this period of his life, either 1824 or 1825, Turner became a fugitive and fled to the woods. Like hundreds of others before him, he quit the plantation because of brutal treatment, in his case a savage flogging by the overseer. He bore the marks of this until the end of his life. A description of Turner that appeared in the Virginia papers before his capture after the rebellion in 1831 ran as follows:

5 ft. 6 or 8 inches high, weighs between 150 and 160 pounds, rather bright complexion, but not a mulatto, broad shoulders, large flat nose, large eyes, broad flat feet, rather knock-kneed, walks brisk and active, hair on the top of the head very thin, no beard, except on the upper lip and the top of the chin, a scar on one of his temples, also on the back of his neck, a large knot on one of the bones of his right arm, near the wrist, produced by a blow.

After he had been gone for nearly thirty days, Turner's

fellow slaves assumed that he had gone for good and that he had made his getaway to the North. But to their amazement he came back one day; and they murmured against him behind his back, saying that if they were as smart as he, "they would not serve any master in the world."

What went on in Nat Turner's mind when he was alone in the Virginia woods? He must undoubtedly have been sorely tempted to flee north just as his father had done before him. Instead, after a fierce inner struggle, he decided to return to slavery. Bound up with this decision—either causing it, or resulting from it—was a vision that he experienced. "About this time," he told Gray,

I had a vision—and I saw white spirits and black spirits engaged in battle, and the sun was darkened—the thunder rolled in the Heavens, and blood flowed in streams —and I heard a voice saying, "Such is your luck, such you are called to see, and let it come rough or smooth, you must surely bear it."

The wild woods which Nat Turner had fled to were more than just a place where a man or woman might hide; traditionally the wilderness was where Americans, white as well as black, turned aside from other men and women to commune with themselves and to seek God. Here, by yourself, you struggled to find the meaning of the world and to fashion a vision of the future. Turner, at this time, was triumphant: he had won his vision, and he would in turn communicate it to others so that they would see it as clearly as he. *There is*, God had told him, *to be a bloody struggle to make black men and women free; you and your comrades are chosen to undertake it.*

Turner returned to his master's plantation in 1825. Outwardly his existence continued much as before. But an extraordinary new dimension had been added to his inner life. He knew now what he had to do—he had to lead and organize his fellow slaves in a struggle for freedom. There was in his mind a tremendous sense of urgency about this assignment; Nat Turner at this time shared with Sinda the conviction that doomsday was at hand, when the dead would rise and God would make the final judgment separating the sheep from the goats, the righteous from the damned. If he, Nat Turner, was indeed to be saved, then he must execute God's will, he must carry out the liberation struggle before the end of the world. He told Gray,

I sought more than ever to obtain true holiness before the great day of judgment should appear. . . . And from the first steps of righteousness until the last, was I made perfect, and the Holy Ghost was with me, and said, "Behold me as I stand in the Heavens."

As he worked in the fields Nat Turner began to look about him for signs that the day of judgment was at hand. Everywhere he found evidence that the end of the world was indeed coming.

There were lights in the sky to which the children of darkness gave other names than what they really were —for they were the lights of the Savior's hands, stretched forth from east to west, even as they were extended on the cross on Calvary for the redemption of sinners.

In the fiery cross extended across the heavens, Turner found the promise of a new redemption, and also of a new crucifixion. Other signs that he saw in the fields as he toiled made this clear to him. Drops of blood glistened upon the standing corn, like bloody dew fallen from heaven, and there were strange signs and characters written in blood upon the leaves of the trees. Turner explained the meaning of these miracles "to many, both white and black, in the neighborhood." Christ, who had shed his blood for sinners, was now laying down the burden that he had borne for man- and womankind; the day of judgment was at hand. "For," he told the wondering people,

as the blood of Christ had been shed on this earth, and had ascended to heaven for the salvation of sinners, and was now returning to earth again in the form of dew— and as the leaves on the trees bore the impression of the figures I had seen in the heavens, it was plain to me that the Savior was about to lay down the yoke he had borne for the sins of men, and the great day of judgment was at hand.

In the time that remained, a black Jesus would replace the white one who laid down his burden, and a black saint would lead his people to redemption. This black Jesus was Nat Turner. First, he took his flock down to the river and baptized them in the sight of a jeering multitude. Then he set in motion plans to go forth into the field of battle and fight the forces of evil. Soon, the Spirit told Turner, the time was at hand; and, said the Spirit,

by signs in the heavens it would make known to me when I should commence the great work—and until the first sign appeared, I should conceal it from the knowl-

edge of men— And on the appearance of the sign . . .
I should arise and prepare myself, and slay my enemies
with their own weapons.

Nat Turner was a patient man. The months passed, and still he waited for a special sign that his time had come. It appeared on February 12, 1831, a partial eclipse of the sun. The fields darkened, the birds stopped singing, the world was quiet. And at once Turner gathered his intimates around him and told them his plan: "The seal," as he said, "was removed from my lips, and I communicated the great work laid out for me to do, to four in whom I had the greatest confidence."

Some people have found it strange that a rebel should wait for a solar eclipse before starting his rebellion. Actually it wasn't strange at all. Until very recently millions of people have been ignorant of the scientific explanation of solar and lunar eclipses. For thousands of years simple and unlettered folk have interpreted these eclipses as an awesome sign of God's judgment, of impending catastrophe. The eclipse, along with such disasters as plagues, earthquakes, or volcanic eruptions, has been seen as a warning of divine punishment, as a sign that the end of the world was at hand.

There was, for example, an eclipse of the sun on January 9, 1777, in the middle of the Revolutionary War, and it caused a panic among the German troops fighting with the British in New Jersey. The patriots made fun of what they called "the ignorant superstition" of the enemy, but many Americans were themselves victims of the same kind of belief. On May 19, 1780, a dark cloud caused by forest fires covered Boston and blotted out the daylight. People were very much afraid, and thought that it was a sign that God was angry with Bostonians; that something terrible was going to happen. "Yesterday," wrote a correspondent of the *Boston Country Journal* on May 20,

we were visited by a most unusual and uncomfortable phenomenon. As early as ten o'clock in the morning, a thick darkness came over the face of the country, so that it was impossible to move about the house without the assistance of a candle. Many persons were much frightened at the sudden darkness, and some thought that judgment-day had come.

So it happened that Nat Turner saw the sign of God in the sky, and knew that his time had come, *the time when the Lord's anointed should rise up, and ungodly men tremble in the sight of the righteous.*

The precise date that Nat Turner set for his revolt was July 4, 1831. Plowman and prophet, he dreamed of a second Declaration of Independence, and it is not idle to think that he may have read the scorching preamble for this Declaration that William Lloyd Garrison had composed and read from a Boston pulpit two short years before, in 1829:

They—the American people—arrogantly styling themselves the champions of freedom, for a long course of years have been guilty of the most cruel and protracted tyranny. They have invaded our territories, depopulated our villages, and kindled among us the flames of an exterminating war. They have wedged us into the holds of their "floating hells" with suffocating compactness, and without distinction of age or sex. . . . They have brought us to a free and Christian land (so-called) and sold us in their market-places like cattle—even in the proud capital of their Union, and within sight of their legislative halls, where tyranny struts in the semblance of liberty. They have cruelly torn the wife from her husband, the mother from her daughter, and children from their parents, and sold them into perpetual exile. They have confined us in loathesome cells and secret prisons— driven us in large droves from state to state, beneath a burning sky, half-naked and heavily manacled. . . . They have compelled us to till their ground, to carry them, to fan them when they sleep, and tremble when they wake, and rewarded us only with stripes, and hunger, and nakedness. They have lacerated our bodies with whips and brands, and knives . . . nor do they esteem it a crime to murder us at will.

But there was a hitch in the plans. It was not until six weeks later that the conspiracy began to be seriously organized. On Sunday, August 20, Henry, Hark, Sam, Nelson, Will, and Jack went out into the woods to prepare supper, and there Nat Turner joined them. After eating a last supper together they agreed upon a plan: They would go from plantation to plantation and kill all the whites they found; they would gather guns and equipment as they went, and they would rally the slaves. No white person was to be spared, regardless of age or sex, "until we had armed and equipped ourselves, and gathered sufficient force."

At about ten o'clock that night the group attacked the home of Joseph Travis, whom Nat Turner described as "a kind master [who] placed the greatest confidence in me . . . I had no cause to complain of his treatment."

Southern woodcut depicting the murder of
Nat Turner's master, Joseph Travis.

The discovery of Nat Turner, 1831.

A ladder was placed against the wall and the conspirators entered the house. The killing of the family, five in all, as Turner said, "was the work of a moment." A search of the house netted four guns, several old muskets, and some powder.

By sunrise on Monday morning three other houses had been invaded and their families put to the axe; in each case the raid was followed by a search for money and weapons. As slaves on the plantations thus attacked joined the rebels, the original group grew in numbers. By the middle of the morning, as the carnage continued, the rebel band rose to fifty or sixty; all had horses and were armed with guns, axes, swords, and clubs.

By midday the alarm had been given, and the news of the uprising spread rapidly. When Turner and his followers attacked the home of James W. Parker, they encountered armed resistance from the whites. This clash was decisive; Turner's band scattered, and he was able to rally only a few of them. Nat Turner hid out for about six weeks in the woods. He was captured at the end of October, long after all the other conspirators had been taken or killed.

Why did Turner conceive, lead, and plan his revolt? As Thomas Gray sat in the jail and took down the story from Turner's own lips, his puzzlement deepened. "It has been said," Gray wrote, "that he was ignorant and cowardly, and that his object was to murder and rob for the purpose of obtaining money to make his escape." This obviously made no sense. Turner had escaped once, and come back of his own free will. Ignorant he certainly was not; not only could he read and write but, as Gray put it, "for natural intelligence and quickness of apprehension he is surpassed by few men I have ever seen."

As for being a coward, it is true that Turner surrendered quietly when he was finally captured. But to Gray this decision to be taken rather than die did not indicate cowardice, but character and determination. "When," wrote Gray, "he saw Mr. Phipps present his gun, he said he knew it was impossible for him to escape as the woods were full of men; he therefore thought it better to surrender, and trust to fortune for his escape."

A recent writer, William Styron, in his *Confessions of Nat Turner*, has provided another explanation. Styron views Turner as a pervert with a brilliant mind, an exceptional person, almost an accident of nature. Gifted with a Napoleonic vision and a formidable personal drive, he had, Styron thinks, little in common with the herd of dumb field workers whom he led.

The trouble with this view of the matter is that there is no evidence for it outside of Styron's imagination. Slave revolts like Turner's were not, as Styron would have us believe, one-in-a-million accidents. On the contrary, they were the inevitable fruit of the southern soil watered with the blood and the tears of its black people. Plantation owners understood this very well—much better, perhaps, than Styron does. Why else the endless struggle to keep black men and women ignorant, isolated, degraded, physically exhausted, and spiritually cowed?

Thomas Gray was a white man who hated and feared Turner, but he took down Turner's words faithfully, and then added his own conclusion: *"They certainly bear the stamp of truth and sincerity."* As he looked at Turner he marveled at:

the calm deliberate composure with which he spoke of
his late deeds and intentions, the expression of his fiend-
like face when excited by enthusiasm, still bearing the
stains of the blood of helpless innocence about him;
clothed with rags and covered with chains; yet daring
to raise his manacled hands to heaven, with a spirit soar-
ing above the attributes of man.

Nat Turner's trial took place in the county seat of
Jerusalem in the first week of November, 1831. The
prisoner was led in and faced the court, standing. Five
magistrates sat upon the bench. The clerk read the indictment that charged him with conspiracy and murder,
crimes against the Commonwealth of Virginia and its
peace.

"How say you, Nat Turner," asked the clerk, "are
you guilty or not guilty?"

"Not guilty," Turner said.

The "confessions" as taken down by Thomas Gray
were introduced in evidence and read to the court.
Turner introduced no further evidence and attempted
no further defense. "I have," as he told the court, "made
a full confession to Mr. Gray, and I have nothing more
to say."

The presiding magistrate, Jeremiah Cobb, pronounced
sentence of death. Turner heard the words unmoved.
He had passed his own judgment upon the world of
slavery; he had called men to redemption, and, long
ago, he had decided to pay the price. He thought of his
death as marking, not failure, not an end to the struggle,
but a beginning. As he himself said to Gray: *Was not
Jesus crucified?*

Nat Turner made the decision to stay in the land of

slavery, to fight the oppressor and, if need be, to die. Hundreds of others made the equally difficult decision to take themselves out of the southland altogether.

I Sought My Lord

I sought my Lord down __ in a wil-der-ness, __
__ In - a wil-der-ness __ In - a wil-der-ness, I
sought my Lord down __ in - a wil-der-ness, For
I'm a - go - in' home.

I found free grace down in a wilderness,
    In a wilderness
    In a wilderness,
I found free grace down in a wilderness,
    For I'm a-goin' home.

My father preaches down in a wilderness,
    In a wilderness
    In a wilderness,
My father preaches down in a wilderness,
    For I'm a-goin' home.

BEFORE THE WIND
Henry Bibb's Flight, 1837

Oh, that I had the wings of a dove, that I might soar away to where there is no slavery, no clanking of chains, no captives, no lacerating of backs, no parting of husbands and wives, and where man ceases to be the property of his fellow man.

Henry Bibb, *Life and Adventures of Henry Bibb*

Throughout the period of our story, the southern newspapers were filled with advertisements for black men, women, and children who had run away. People were described by sex, age, height, weight, clothing, hair, speech, skin color, but above all by the mutilations they had suffered or the scars that they bore. Here is one such advertisement, typical of thousands:

$100 Reward

RANAWAY from my plantation, in Bolivar County, Mississippi, a negro man named MAY, aged 40 years, 5 feet 10 or 11 inches high, copper colored, and very straight; his front teeth are good, and stand a little open; stout through the shoulders, and has some scars on his back that show above the skin plain, caused by the whip; he frequently hiccups when eating, if he has not got water handy; he was pursued into Ozark County, Mo., and there left. I will give the above reward for his confinement in jail, so that I can get him.

James H. Cousar
(Jefferson Inquirer,
November 27, 1852)

Sheriffs, too, or constables, caught runaways, held them in the local jail, and advertised for the owner to pick up his property. Slaves unclaimed within three months or some such period were sold at public auction, and the proceeds used to pay the jailer's costs and advertising. Here is a typical jailer's ad:

Committed

To the jail of Choctaw County [Alabama], by Judge Young, a RUNAWAY SLAVE, who calls his name BILLY, and says he belongs to the late William Johnson, and was in the employment of John Jones, near Alexandria, La. He is about 5 feet 10 inches high, black, about 40 years old, much scarred on the face and head, and quite intelligent. The owner is requested to come forward, prove his property, and take him from Jail, or he will be disposed of according to law.

(Alabama Standard,
November 29, 1852)

There were differences between runaways from plantations in the Deep South and runaways from the border states—that belt of states close to or bordering on the North which included Virginia, Delaware, Maryland, Kentucky, Tennessee, and Missouri. These differences we may think of as fundamental to understanding the whole history of the struggle against slavery.

While it is true that some fugitives from the Deep South headed for the North, most did not. The distances to be covered were too great, the obstacles to be overcome too formidable, the chances of making it, too slight. Many Deep South slaves who fled did not go very far or stay out very long. Bayous, swamps, woods, or caves were their refuge. The master might go hunting runaways himself, or hire somebody else to do so, usually with dogs. If the slave, like May or Billy, was captured in a slave community far from his starting point, the master's problem was minimal. All he had to do was to "prove his property" in some fashion acceptable to the local authority holding the slave, pay whatever charges and rewards were due, pick up the fugitive, and drag him home.

But in the border states it was possible for many more slaves than in the Deep South to play for the high stakes of total release from the slavery empire, for liberty itself. Though the risks were still great, as we shall see, it was not too difficult a matter for border state slaves, with a little help from their friends, to cross over into the free states. Between 1800 and 1860 border state slave owners lost several thousand black workers in this way.

These fugitives were conducting a struggle against slavery quite as much as people like Nat Turner, though their rebellion took a different form. The act of flight itself asserted a fundamental right that had been set forth originally in the Declaration of Independence.

In its preamble the Declaration stated that all men— and, one would suppose, women too—are endowed with an inalienable right to "life, liberty and the pursuit of happiness." But you cannot always "pursue" something by staying in the same place; often you have to move, and if you don't find what you are looking for in one place, you have the right to move to another. Thus the pursuit of happiness involves, logically and inevitably, a right of movement. This right fugitive slaves were exercising to the limit. By the act of locomotion they were asserting and demanding their right to liberty; speaking with their feet they were stating that freedom could only be won, and only defended—by moving.

American slaves were here boldly asserting and seizing hold of their fundamental rights as human beings, and this was to have tremendously important consequences for the unfolding of the struggle against slavery. *It was the fugitive who first summoned the North to challenge the slave power,* to battle that power, not on all fronts, but for one seemingly small cause: the legal and constitutional rights of the tiny minority who dared ferry the broad Ohio or tramp through woods and fields across the Mason-Dixon line.

Henry Bibb, of Shelby County, Kentucky, was one of the many border state slaves who fled the South. He made his first trip north in 1837, six years after the death of Nat Turner. Bibb became active in the anti-slavery movement and published his *Narrative of the Life and Adventures of Henry Bibb* in 1850. It is the story of a man who made frantic efforts to liberate not just himself but his family as well. For this purpose he returned to the South several times, exposing himself repeatedly to the risk of savage punishment and re-enslavement.

Born in 1815, Bibb never knew his father. He was torn away from his mother while still a child, and hired

A runaway slave.

out to work for different farmers. In this way he learned soon enough what it meant to be a slave. "I have often worked," he wrote,

without half enough to eat, both late and early, by day and by night. I have often laid my wearied limbs down at night to rest upon a dirt floor, or a bench, without any covering at all. . . . I have also been compelled in early life, to go at the bidding of a tyrant, through all kinds of weather, hot or cold, wet or dry, and without shoes frequently, until the month of December, with my bare feet on the cold frosty ground, cracked open and bleeding as I walked.

Like dozens of other border state slaves, Bibb was tormented by the sight of free soil and the passion for freedom that it kindled. Standing on the Ohio River bluffs he watched the gaily painted steamboats as they glided up and down the stream; he gazed northward into the blue sky and dreamed that he was in Canada. Truly, he told himself, there is nothing in all creation that is lower or more miserable than a slave. "I thought," he wrote, "of the fishes of the water, the fowls of the air, the wild beasts of the forest; all appeared to be free, to go just where they pleased, and I was an unhappy slave!"

In 1833, when he was eighteen years old, Bibb resolved that he would cross the "impassable gulf" of the Ohio and strike out for freedom. Just when he had finally decided to leave, he met Malinda, an Oldham County slave. The two fell in love and decided to get married.

This decision created a problem for the young people,

because, as Bibb pointed out, "a slave marrying according to law is a thing unknown in the history of American slavery." In the eyes of the law no such thing as a permanent, stable slave family had any right to exist. This, of course, was no accident, but a matter of calculated policy on the part of the slave-owning class.

During the early years of the United States, the family played as important a role as it does today. From birth to puberty it was the central influence in a child's life. It protected, clothed, fed, and educated him. It gave him love. It taught him skills, such as farming or a craft. It taught him his identity—who he was, where he and his folks came from. It launched him upon the world.

If the family was this important for white Americans, how much more crucial a role ought it to have played in the lives of black Americans! Black people had been torn forcibly from Africa, and their tribal and family organizations had been shattered or left behind. In facing the harsh American world they would need—much more than whites—the protection of whatever new family ties they could create.

But the family, after all, is a form of social organization. It gives its members protection; it endows them with the power to struggle; it knits them with a bond of blood; and it endows them, when necessary, with a passion for revenge. Of course, slaveholders desired none of this. On one level, they recognized the black family as a stable unit that promoted a high birth rate. On another level, they did their best to destroy the black family, to deny its very existence. Slaves had no right to marriage; they were put together to breed, and torn apart again if

The separation of mother and child.

they didn't. Usually a mating couple just jumped over a broom, and that was it. There might, of course, be a marriage party, but there was no religious ceremony; and, even if there *was* such a ceremony, the most important part got left out. Augustus Ladson, who was born in the Sea Islands in 1826, said: "No minister nebber say, in readin' de matrimony, *let no man put asunder* 'cause a couple would be married tonight and tomorrow one would be taken away and sold."

The daily destruction of family ties as human beings were bought or sold by their masters forms one of the most tormented chapters in the history of slavery. The full force of this agony fell upon the children. "I'se seen de slave speculator," said Henry Grant of South Carolina, "cut de little nigger chillen with keen leather whips, 'cause they'd cry and run after de wagon dat was takin' their mammies away after they was sold." When a parent died, there was no right even to say good-bye if such ceremony stole time from field work. Sarah Gudger, born in North Carolina in 1807, remembered to the end of her life the time when her mother died:

I went to de house and I say to Ole Missie: "My mother she die today. I want to see my mother afore dey puts her away," but she look mean at me and say: "Get on out of here, and get back to work afore I wallop you good." So I went back to my work, with the tears streamin' down my face, just a-ringin' my hands, I wanted to see my mammy so.

Thus, when Henry Bibb and Malinda got "married," there was no marriage license, no marriage ceremony, just a wedding party.

Bibb belonged to one master and his wife to another. This meant that after the two were "married" they must part again and live separately, he on one plantation, she on another. They could visit together only on weekends, and then only for a few brief hours. "I was permitted," wrote Bibb, "to visit her only on Saturday nights, after my work was done, and I had to be home before sunrise on Monday mornings, or take a flogging."

Soon William Gatewood, Malinda's owner, bought Henry too. Bibb at first was overjoyed with this development, but he soon found that the situation was now more unbearable than before. His wife, like so many women on the plantations, was subject daily to physical abuse and sexual outrage. Henry Bibb's manhood was insulted and trampled upon because he saw this happen *and yet was able to do nothing about it.* He wrote:

To live where I must be an eyewitness to her insults, scourgings, and abuses, such as are common to be inflicted upon slaves, was more than I could bear. If my wife must be exposed to the insults and licentious passions of wicked overseers and drivers; if she must bear the stripes of the lash laid on by an unmerciful tyrant . . . Heaven forbid that I should be compelled to witness the sight.

The birth of a little girl in 1834 only added to the father's unhappiness. The baby, Frances, had to be left by both parents as they toiled in the field, "to creep under the feet of an unmerciful old mistress whom I have known to slap . . . little Frances, for crying after her mother, until her little face was left black and blue." Frances was just one more human being dearer to Henry

Bibb than life itself, and whom he was powerless to protect.

Late in 1837 Henry Bibb made the difficult decision to leave his family and strike out for Canada. His intention was to find the way there, get a job, save money, and come back to fetch Malinda and Frances as soon as he could. He was terribly torn. On the one hand, he said, "The voice of liberty was thundering in my very soul, 'Be free, oh man! be free.'" On the other hand,

I was struggling against a thousand obstacles which had clustered around my mind to bind my wounded spirit still in the dark prison of mental degradation. My strong attachments to friends and relatives, with all the love of home and birth-place which is so natural among the human family, twined about my heart and were hard to break away from.

Next to love of family and home, the most powerful force acting to discourage Bibb's flight was the fear that was always present in a slave's life. He was tormented, he tells us, by

the fear of being pursued with guns and bloodhounds, and of being killed, or captured and taken to the extreme South, to linger out my days in hopeless bondage on some sugar or cotton plantation.

But Henry Bibb's mind was made up. He took a tearful leave of his wife and child, had himself ferried across the Ohio to Madison, Indiana, and boarded a steamboat for Cincinnati. He did this in fear and trembling. The mere fact that he was black and traveling alone was a suspicious matter. Any white man who felt inclined had the right to seize and bind him, and send him back to captivity. The officers on these river ships, in addition, kept a sharp lookout for black runaways; the ship's owners were themselves liable to a legal suit, and the award of heavy damages against them, if it could be proved that they had conveyed a fugitive to a free port.

Bibb's skin was light-colored, and he was lucky to escape without challenge. After an all-night trip the ship docked at Cincinnati, which at that time was the biggest city in the Midwest, with a large community of free black people. Bibb met an old black street worker, Job Dundy, who put him in touch with antislavery people. They took him in, fed him, and started him on his way north toward Canada.

Henry Bibb was now in a free state, the state of Ohio. But his deep fear of slavery did not leave him, nor did the feeling of being alone in a hostile world among hostile people. "I travelled on," he tells us,

until I had arrived at the place where I was directed to call on an Abolitionist, but I made no stop: so great were my fears of being pursued by the pro-slavery hunting dogs of the South. I prosecuted my journey vigorously for nearly forty-eight hours without food or rest . . . not knowing what moment I might be captured while travelling among strangers, through cold and fear, breasting the north winds, being thinly clad, pelted by the snow storms through the dark hours of the night, and not a house in which I could enter to shelter me from the storm.

Why did Henry Bibb continue to be afraid? Even though a slave fled the South and took refuge in the free states, it did not follow either that he was free or beyond the reach of his master. On the contrary. Under federal law slave owners had the *right* to search for fugitives in the free states, seize them, manacle them, and drag them back into slavery.

The right to retrieve slaves who fled to the free states was important enough to the slaveholders that they had had it written into the Constitution. The fugitive slave clause was drawn up and introduced at the Philadelphia Convention of 1787 by Pierce Butler himself, and it was adopted with little debate or opposition from the free-state delegates. Article IV, clause 2, of the Constitution became known as "the fugitive felon and slave clause." The part of it relating to fugitive slaves read as follows:

No person held to service or labor in one state, under the laws thereof, escaping into another, shall, in consequence of any law or regulation therein, be discharged from such service or labor, but shall be delivered up on claim of the party to whom such service or labor may be due.

This very general statement purposely avoided the use of the word "slave," but its meaning was clear enough to fugitives like Henry Bibb. From his point of view the clause might be translated as follows:

If Henry Bibb is a slave under Kentucky law and he flees to Ohio, where slavery is banned by Ohio law, he shall not become a free man, but he must be surrendered to his owner when his owner claims him.

By 1837, when Henry Bibb fled from Kentucky, most northern states, including Ohio, had outlawed slavery.

If Article IV, clause 2, of the federal Constitution had not existed, a slave entering Ohio would have been made free by the mere act of crossing the state line. This clause made a big difference: it forbade northern states to liberate hunted slaves who sought refuge within their borders. On the contrary, such states were constitutionally bound to surrender fugitives to the slaveholders and their hunting dogs on demand. This was the reason for the fear that gripped Henry Bibb as he worked his way north toward Canada.

All that winter Henry Bibb remained in Ohio, working and saving money so that he might return to Kentucky and rescue his family. Going back in the spring of 1838 he was recognized, seized, and shipped south. But Bibb succeeded in getting away from his captors at Louisville, and at once headed back to Bedford, where his family was. "I travelled all that night," he tells us,

guided on my way by the stars alone. The next morning just before the break of day, I came right to a large plantation about which I secreted myself, until the darkness of the next night began to disappear. The morning larks began to chirp and sing merrily, pretty soon I heard the whip crack, and the voice of the ploughman driving in the cornfield. About breakfast time, I heard the sound of the horn; saw a number of slaves in the field with a white man, whom I supposed to be their overseer. He started to the house before the slaves, which gave me an opportunity to get the attention of one of the slaves, whom I met at the fence . . . and made known to him my wants and distresses.

The slave to whom Bibb talked gave him bread, and

The capture of a fugitive slave.

in return Bibb gave him information on how to get to Canada. When he himself arrived back in Bedford, he found that the alarm had been raised, and his family was being watched. It was beyond his power to rescue them, and there was nothing left to do except say good-bye and leave. "One morning," wrote Bibb,

about 2 o'clock, I took my leave of my little family and started for Canada. This was almost like tearing off the limbs from my body. When we were about to separate, Malinda clasped my hand exclaiming, "oh my soul! my heart is almost broken at the thought of this dangerous separation. This may be the last time we shall ever see each other's faces in this life, which will destroy all my future prospects of life and happiness forever."At this time the poor unhappy woman burst into tears and wept loudly; and my eyes were not dry. We separated with the understanding that she was to wait until the excitement was all over; after which she was to meet me at a certain place in the State of Ohio; which would not be longer than two months from that time.

Bibb once more was successful in getting away to Ohio, but Malinda was unable to find a way to join her husband. Again he came back to Kentucky to try and rescue her, and again he was taken prisoner, chained, and sold to the Deep South. After many trials and adventures he escaped and found his way to Canada. But all Bibb's efforts to locate his wife and child proved in vain. After 1845, he never heard of Malinda or Frances again.

In his repeated flights north through Ohio and Michigan, Henry Bibb followed a track used by many fugitives from the South. These trails to freedom—in the Mid-

Henry Bibb.

west, New York State, and New England—have been collectively labeled "the Underground Railroad." The story of how black people traveled these trails, and how they were helped along the way by antislavery people, has become an American legend.

As with many legends, it is not easy to separate fact from fiction in the Underground Railroad. Unselfish and dedicated white people without doubt gave help to the black fugitives. But it is likely that the story has grown in the telling; there is an element of self-serving fiction in the picture of heroic whites taking the helpless and oppressed blacks by the hand, hiding and feeding them, and moving them onward toward the land of freedom. It is more important to bear in mind that, first and foremost, black people helped themselves. Few acts of courage and defiance committed by whites in support of fugitives ever equaled the courage and defiance that the act of flight *itself* demanded. Black people, too, not only helped themselves, they also helped each other—this becomes quite clear from Bibb's *Narrative* and from many others. Thousands of such acts as the giving of bread in the corn field must have occurred, but history does not know of them and has not recorded them.

Slave owners who sought to recapture runaways were not always too particular about finding and dragging back the *same* man or woman that had escaped. This meant problems and suffering for free black people in the North.

Oh, Freedom

fore I'll be a slave I'll lie bur-ied in my grave, And go home to my Lord and_ be_ free.

No more moaning, no more moaning,
No more moaning over me;
And before I'll be a slave,
I'll lie buried in my grave,
And go home to my Lord, and be free.

No more mourning, no more mourning,
No more mourning over me;
And before I'll be a slave, etc.

No more weeping, no more weeping,
No more weeping over me;
And before I'll be a slave, etc.

No more sighing, no more sighing,
No more sighing over me;
And before I'll be a slave, etc.

Oh, what singing, oh, what singing,
Oh, what singing over me;
And before I'll be a slave, etc.

Oh, what shouting, oh, what shouting,
Oh, what shouting over me;
And before I'll be a slave, etc.

Oh, freedom! Oh freedom!
Oh, freedom over me;
And before I'll be a slave, etc.

THE SELLING OF SOLOMON
The Agony of Solomon Northup, 1841–1854

Behold, I have dreamed a dream more; and behold, the sun and the moon and the eleven stars made obeisance to me.

Joseph, son of Israel

Until the outbreak of the Civil War, slaves were in scarce supply. Not all the breeding activities that the masters encouraged were enough to meet the swelling demand. The price of an able-bodied unskilled male slave rose from about $600 in the 1820s to about $1500 in the 1850s. Until the end of the period, people continued to be kidnaped in Africa and smuggled illegally into the South.

Given this scarcity, and the high price of slaves, it is not surprising that slave traders looked to the northern United States, as well as to Africa, to replenish the slave supply. Slaves escaped *to* the North; the system recouped its losses by taking black people *from* the North. A lucrative trade arose in kidnaping black men and women, dragging them across state lines, and selling them to owners and traders in the South. This was an easy matter so long as northerners showed no disposition to challenge Article IV, clause 2, of the Constitution, which gave slave owners the right to seize fugitives wherever they might find them. The existence of the fugitive slave clause became a *screen* behind which hundreds of free and innocent people were seized and delivered into perpetual servitude. The presumption, after all, was that a black person being taken south in chains was a fugitive.

Few black people seized in the North and sold into slavery ever found their way home again to tell the tale. Solomon Northup was one of these few fortunates; he wrote the story of his experiences and published it under the title *Twelve Years a Slave* in 1853. This work is one of the most important testimonies about slavery that we have; it was written by a kidnap victim directly following the searing experience he had undergone. It casts a bright light upon the horrible reality of the seizure and enslavement of citizens of the northern states.

Solomon Northup, a free man, was born at Minerva, Essex County, New York, in 1808. He was the son of a New York slave, Mintus Northup, who had been freed by his owner upon his death. Mintus Northup did well in freedom, worked hard as a farmer, and acquired enough land to entitle him to vote. Solomon and his brother, Joseph, grew up helping their father on the farm; Solomon himself was an avid reader of books and also played the violin, which he described as "the ruling passion of my youth."

In 1829 Mintus Northup died on the family farm not far from Fort Edward. That same year Solomon married Anne Hampton and they set up housekeeping together in "the old yellow building then standing at the southern extremity of Fort Edward village . . . known as the Fort House." In 1830 Northup worked on repairing the Champlain Canal; and in 1831 he set himself up in the business of hauling rafts of timber along the canal by horse from Lake Champlain to Troy, hiring several workers to assist him. When the waters froze in the early winter of that year, Northup took to lumbering. Then, in the spring of 1832, he rented land at Kingsbury, north of the village of Sandy Hill, bought a pair of oxen, planted corn, and began to farm "upon as large a scale as my utmost means would permit."

When winter came again, Northup and his wife were not idle. He played his violin at young people's parties, and she, a fine cook, worked at a hotel. "With fiddling, cooking, and farming," he wrote, "we soon found ourselves in possession of abundance." But in the spring of 1833, for reasons he does not give, the couple abandoned their farm and moved to Saratoga Springs. Northup found a house in town for them to live in, and worked at various jobs, including railroad construction and driving a hack.

There, in Saratoga Springs, the family remained until 1841. By that time the Northups were the parents of three children, Elizabeth, Margaret, and Alonzo, youngsters whose voices, as their father wrote, "were music in our ears."

One day in March 1841 two respectably dressed men accosted Northup on the street in Saratoga Springs and entered into conversation with him. They said that they were with a circus then playing in Washington, D.C., and were at that time touring for a while on their own; and they offered him a job playing the fiddle at their "exhibitions." Northup liked the idea—it would fill the time until the Saratoga season opened a little later in the year. So he accepted the strangers' offer and went off with them without even bothering to inform his wife, who had gone over to Sandy Hill, some twenty miles away, to cook at the hotel while the county court was in session. Northup evidently felt that he would be back home again before the family was. The two strangers took Northup to New York City, and then persuaded him to go on with them as far as Washington. Evidently he did not need much persuasion; he had never been so far from home before in his life, he had never seen such interesting sights, and he was being well paid in the bargain.

After arriving in Washington on April 6, the trio visited the Capitol and then went off to witness the funeral of President William Henry Harrison, who died on April 4, just one month after his inauguration. "The roar of the cannon and the tolling of bells," wrote Northup,

filled the air, while many houses were shrouded with crepe, and the streets black with people. As the day advanced, the procession made its appearance . . . carriage after carriage, in long succession, while thousands upon thousands followed on foot—all moving to the sound of melancholy music.

During the day, Northup's new-found friends plied him from time to time with drink. In the evening he became very ill and eventually lost consciousness. When he came to he found he was "alone, in utter darkness, and in chains," confined in Williams' slave pen, which was only a stone's throw from the Capitol that the young New Yorker had visited the day before.

After a while, James H. Birch, a Washington slave dealer, arrived, and informed Northup "that I was his slave—that he had bought me, and that he was about to send me to New Orleans." Northup, no doubt like hundreds of others kidnaped in this way, insisted that he was no slave, but a free man:

> I asserted, aloud and boldly, that I was a free man—a resident of Saratoga, where I had a wife and children, who were also free, and that my name was Northup. . . . Again and again I asserted that I was no man's slave, and insisted upon his taking off my chains at once.

Birch flew into a rage and "with blasphemous oaths called me a black liar, a runaway from Georgia." He proceeded to make entirely clear to Northup what the consequences would be if he continued to claim his freedom. Birch threw his victim over a bench, face down, and rained blow after blow upon his back with a paddle, "a piece of hardwood board, eighteen or twenty inches long, moulded to the shape of an old-fashioned pudding stick, or ordinary oar." From time to time he stopped to catch his breath, repeating the same question: "Do you still say that you are a free man?" Northup continued to give the same answer. "All his brutal blows," he wrote, "could not force from my lips the foul lie that I was a slave."

Finally the paddle broke. Birch threw it away and began to flog his victim with a length of rope. At last Northup broke down and screamed for mercy. If his sufferings had been great before, now they were like "the burning agonies of hell." But the beating went on and

A slave-coffle passing the Capital,
an 1820 engraving.

on. "A man with a particle of mercy in his soul," said Northup, "would not have beaten a dog so cruelly."

Finally the torture ended and Birch left. Northup remained locked in his cell and alone for several days. Sometimes sleep came in spite of the burning pain in his back, and he dreamed of Anne and their children,

dreamed I was again in Saratoga—that I could see their faces, and hear their voices calling me. Awakening from the pleasant phantasms of sleep to the bitter realities around me, I could but groan and weep.

After two weeks Birch marched Northup, along with other captives, through the streets of Washington, and took them to Richmond, Virginia, by boat and stage. There Northup was handcuffed to another kidnap victim, named Robert. "Like myself," said Northup,

he had been born free, and had a wife and two children in Cincinnati. He said he had come south with two men, who had hired him [in Cincinnati]. Without free papers, he had been seized at Fredericksburg, placed in confinement, and beaten until he had learned, as I had, the necessity and the policy of silence.

Then the group was placed on board a brig, the *Orleans,* bound south. When they reached Norfolk more slaves were brought aboard, among them another kidnap victim named Arthur. He had been attacked by a gang on a lonely street, overpowered, beaten unconscious, and dragged to the slavepen. But for him the story ended happily. When the brig docked at New Orleans two men came up and called out "Arthur!" They were friends who had come all the way from Norfolk to rescue him after his kidnapers had been arrested and thrown in jail.

As for Northup and the others, they were met on arrival by Theophilus Freeman, Birch's partner, marched through the streets, and lodged once more in a slave pen. "Could it be possible," Northup thought as he wrapped his blanket around him that night,

that I was thousands of miles from home—that I had been driven through the streets like a dumb beast—that I had been chained and beaten without mercy—that I was even then herded with a drove of slaves, a slave myself?

Next day Theophilus Freeman prepared his shipment for sale. All had to wash, and the men to shave. Hat, coat, shirt, pants, and shoes were issued to the men, calico frocks and kerchiefs to the women. Freeman had announced the arrival of this new consignment by inserting an advertisement in the local papers, like the following:

JUST RECEIVED

Forty very likely young NEGROES, *consisting of field hands, mechanics, seamstresses, house servants, etc., and for sale, for cash or good city paper.*

Soon customers began to call at the pen. The slaves were made to walk up and down so that they might be inspected. Prospective buyers, added Northup,

would feel of our hands and arms and bodies, turn us about, ask us what we could do, make us open our mouths and show our teeth, precisely as a jockey examines a horse. . . . Sometimes a man or woman was taken back to the small house in the yard, stripped, and inspected more minutely. Scars upon a slave's back were considered evidence of a rebellious or unruly spirit, and hurt his sale.

At Freeman's pen Northup witnessed an event that happened sometimes at public slave sales and auctions: the splitting up of a family. Eliza, a young slave woman who had come with the group from Virginia, had two little children, Emily and Randall. Both were taken from her and sold. When Randall was sold, Northup tells us,

Eliza burst into a paroxysm of grief, weeping plaintively. Freeman turned around to her, savagely, with his whip in his uplifted hand, ordering her to stop her noise, or he would flog her. He would not have such work, such snivelling; and unless she ceased that minute, he would take her into the yard and give her a hundred lashes.

Over and over Eliza begged Freeman not to part her from her child, over and over begged the purchaser to buy her along with Randall. It was no use, Randall must go alone: "Then Eliza ran to him; embraced him passionately; kissed him again and again; told him to remember her—all the while her tears falling in the boy's face like rain." Randall tried to console his mother. "Don't cry, mama," he said, "I will be a good boy."

Eliza, Northup, and several other slaves were bought by a wealthy planter called William Ford, and taken up the Mississippi by boat to the parish of Avoyelles on the Red River. Northup thought himself lucky in this, his first master, whom he described as "a kind, noble, candid

Christian man . . . fortunate was the slave who came to his possession."

Northup was set to work at the wood mill, piling lumber that had to be loaded onto wagons and sent for sale to the town of Lamourie. Northup soon figured that delivery would be far less costly if it was sent by water rather than by land. He set to work removing obstructions to navigation on the creek, built a raft, and took a load of lumber to town by water. "From this time," he relates, "control of bringing the lumber to Lamourie was placed in my hands until the contract was fulfilled."

Working for William Ford, Northup enjoyed such happiness as a slave might know; but this pleasant situation did not last for more than a few months. Ford fell into debt and had to sell slaves to meet the demands of his creditors. Northup was among those sold; he became the property of John Tibbets, a carpenter, and began to work as Tibbets' assistant. This marked the beginning of real hardship in his life as a slave:

I was now compelled to labor very hard. From earliest day until late at night, I was not allowed to be a moment idle. Notwithstanding, Tibbets was never satisfied. He was continually cursing and complaining. He never spoke to me a kind word. I was his faithful slave, and earned him high wages every day, and yet I went to my cabin nightly, loaded with abuse and stinging epithets.

Tibbets evidently took an instant dislike to his slave. Matters came to a head when he wished to flog Northup, and Northup resisted. Some time later Tibbets, seeking to be revenged for this humiliation, tried to kill Northup while the two were at work.

SOLOMON IN HIS PLANTATION SUIT.

Solomon Northup.

His anger grew more and more violent, until, finally, with an oath, such a bitter, frightful oath as only Tibbets could utter, he seized a hatchet from the work-bench and darted toward me, swearing he would cut my head open. It was a matter of life or death. The sharp, bright blade of the hatchet glittered in the sun. In another instant it would be buried in my brain, and yet in that instant . . . I reasoned with myself. If I stood still, my doom was certain; if I fled, ten chances to one the hatchet, flying from his hand with a too-deadly and un-erring aim, would strike me in the back. There was but one course to take. Springing toward him with all my power, and meeting him fullhalf-way, before he could bring down the blow, with one hand I caught his up-lifted arm, with the other seized him by the throat.

In this situation Northup faced the dilemma with which a slave attacked by his master was always confronted. If he resisted, he would be killed for resisting; if he failed to resist, he would die anyway. "I dared not murder him," as he put it, "and I dared not let him live."

In a moment Northup's mind was made up: he decided to flee to the swamps. Tibbets was after him soon enough. "Looking up the bayou," he wrote,

I saw Tibbets and two others on horseback, coming at a fast gait, followed by a troop of dogs. There were as many as eight or ten. Distant as I was, I knew them. They belonged on the adjoining plantation. The dogs used on Bayou Boeuf for hunting slaves are a kind of blood-hound, but a far more savage breed than is found in the Northern States. They will attack a Negro, at their master's bidding, and cling to him as the common bull-dog will cling to a four-footed animal. Frequently their loud baying is heard in the swamps. . . .

Deeper and deeper Northup retreated into the bayou. He was in "the great Pacoudrie Swamp":

It was filled with immense trees—the sycamore, the gum, the cotton wood and cypress, and extends, I am informed, to the shores of the Calcasieu river. For thirty or forty miles it is without inhabitants, save wild beasts— the bear, the wild-cat, the tiger, and great slimy reptiles, that are crawling through it everywhere.

The sun went down, the moon rose. Northup still stumbled on amid waters that came at times above his knees. "My clothes," he wrote,

were in tatters, my hands, face, and body covered with scratches, received from the sharp knots of fallen trees, and in climbing over piles of brush and floodwood. My bare foot was full of thorns. I was besmeared with mud and muck, and the green slime that had collected on the surface of the dead water, in which I had been immersed to the neck many times during the day and night.

Hour after hour Northup trudged on through the night, making a huge circle in the swamps as he traveled first south and then northwest, until he reached the high ground of the pinewoods where his first master, William Ford, lived. He arrived at the house at eight o'clock in the morning.

Ford and his wife welcomed the fugitive kindly, listened to his story attentively, and gave him food, including a bowl of milk and dainties that a slave would rarely, if ever, have the privilege of tasting. As Northup relates:

I was hungry, I was weary, but neither food nor rest afforded me half the pleasure as did the blessed voices speaking kindness and consolation. It was the oil and wine with which the Good Samaritan in the Great Pine Woods was ready to pour into the wounded spirit of the slave, who came to him, stripped of his raiment and half-dead.

After resting a while, Northup strolled into the mistress's garden.

Roses were blooming there, and the long luxuriant vines creeping over the frames. The crimson and golden fruit hung half hidden amidst the younger and older blossoms of the peach, the orange, the plum, and the pomegranate . . . for three days I was diligent in the garden, cleaning the walks, weeding the flower beds, and pulling up the rank grass beneath the jessamine vines. . . . That little paradise in the Great Pine Woods was the oasis in the desert, toward which my heart turned lovingly, during many years of bondage.

Ford had words with Tibbets. Using hatchets and axes on slaves, said he, was shameful; it would set them all to running away, "the swamps will be full of them." Northup did not receive the usual lashing—500 lashes— for running off to the swamp, but was hired out to a man named Eldret to help him clear the wilderness where he planned to start a farm. Here Northup played the role of the typical pioneer, building cabins and cutting down the virgin forest. It is interesting to note that when slaves were used to clear the wilderness, women wielded the axe and did the same work as men. "In the course of two weeks," wrote Northup,

four black girls came down from Eldret's plantation— Charlotte, Fanny, Cresia and Nelly. They were all large and stout. Axes were put into their hands, and they were sent out with Sam and myself to cut trees. They were excellent choppers, the largest oak or sycamore standing but a brief season before their heavy and well-directed blows. At piling logs, they were equal to any man. There are lumberwomen as well as lumbermen in the forests of the South. In fact, in the region of the Bayou Boeuf they perform their share of all the labor required on the plantation. They plough, drag, drive team, clear wild lands, work on the highway, and so forth.

Northup worked at Eldret's for several weeks and then received permission to return to Ford's plantation and visit his friends. The pass that he carried with him read as follows:

Platt [this was the name that Birch and Freeman had given Northup] has permission to go to Ford's planta-tion, on Bayou Boeuf, and return by Tuesday morning.
John M. Tibbetts

This pass system was used throughout the South and played an important part in controlling the movement of black people and capturing fugitives. Any slave found off his master's plantation had to have a valid pass signed by owner or overseer; and he was obliged to produce it for the inspection of any white man who demanded to see it. A slave caught without a pass could be seized,

The reunion of Solomon Northup and his family.

whipped, and lodged in jail. Poor whites thought of stray black people without passes as a godsend: finders of runaways were allowed fees for their services in effecting recapture.

In addition, wherever slaves were numerous, whites were organized to patrol the roads and slave settlements by night. The purpose of such patrols was to catch runaways, prevent illegal movements of black people, and break up illegal assemblies. Patrolers might flog a black person on the road whether he had a pass or not, for the job was a dull one. They even invaded plantations and indulged in their own private lynchings.

After working at Eldrets, Northup was sold to a cotton planter named Epps. For ten years he labored in the cotton fields, being hired out during the harvest season to sugar planters for cane cutting and sugar making. Northup won some relief from field work because of his skill as a fiddle player; he was much in demand at parties, and also played at the "Christmas suppers" that the Bayou Boeuf planters gave once a year for their slaves. "Had it not been for my beloved violin," he wrote, "I scarcely can conceive how I could have endured the long years of bondage." And from the tips which Northup received when he played for white people, he furnished his cabin with pipes, tobacco, and extra shoes.

In 1852 a carpenter named Bass came to do construction work on the Epps plantation. Northup discovered that Bass was a kindly man with a detestation of slavery. So he revealed to Bass his true identity and enlisted his help in writing to his previous employers or associates at Saratoga Springs. When the letter arrived, these people contacted a Sandy Hill attorney, Henry Northup, and he was appointed by the governor of New York as an agent authorized to search for Solomon Northup and secure his return from Louisiana.

Thus it came about that Northup was rescued by his friends and reunited with his family in January 1853. He died a few years later, worn out by his time of sorrow and toil, without ever having received one cent in compensation for his labors, or for the sufferings and wrongs that had been inflicted upon him.

Before Northup died—within four months, in fact, of his returning home—he put the story of his experiences on paper. By 1854 *Twelve Years a Slave* had sold 25,000 copies. Many white northerners, by that time, had become deeply concerned about the fact of southern slavery and the menace that it presented to the survival of the Republic.

BEHOLD, THIS DREAMER COMETH
William Lloyd Garrison, July 4, 1829

Behold this dreamer cometh. Come now therefore, and let us slay him.

Book of Genesis

The struggle against slavery began with the black people who were its immediate victims. For many years, these people waged their own war against the system, while northerners went about their business more or less unaware of the swift, silent revolution taking place in the South, and heedless of the sufferings thus inflicted on its black victims. Gradually, as time passed, white people throughout the North began uneasily to realize that an empire of slavery was coming into being. Few at first, then in growing numbers, white people found themselves making common cause with the slaves and resisting the demands of the slaveholders. This new and spreading resistance took many different forms, and it climaxed in the military struggle of the Civil War.

Many white people who became involved in the movement against slavery were concerned primarily with the menace of the southern system to the survival of a democratic republic. But the vanguard of the antislavery movement—free black people as well as whites—was concerned mainly with the right of black people to full freedom in American society. They were looked upon as radicals in their own time, and were called abolitionists. It is the appearance of this radical abolitionist movement, and its impact upon the country, that will concern us in the present chapter.

The long struggle for the slaves to be free, not merely as *people*, but also as *Americans*, to enjoy the same constitutional rights and protections as any white citizen, is called the civil rights movement. The struggle goes on to this day. For northern whites, it began in a Boston church on July 4, 1829, when a young man of twenty-four wearing wire-rimmed glasses rose to address the congregation. His name was William Lloyd Garrison and he had been born at Newburyport, Massachusetts, in 1805. While still in his teens, Garrison was apprenticed to a Newburyport printer; he educated himself by devouring all the books he could beg, borrow, or buy, which ended up in a pile in his tiny attic room. Now, in July 1829, he was traveling south to become the editor of a Baltimore antislavery newspaper, the *Genius of Universal Emancipation*. Edward Beecher, pastor of the Park Street Church, offered the young man on his way through Boston the opportunity to deliver a Fourth of July address from his pulpit. So here was Garrison, on this bright summer day, getting up in front of a well-dressed Boston audience. Among those sitting in front of the young man was Harriet Beecher, Edward Beecher's sister, who was at that time a schoolteacher. She had just passed her eighteenth birthday.

If the audience expected the usual patriotic address, they must have been both surprised and shocked as the young orator's lucid, burning words fell upon their ears. "The Fourth of July," he told them, "is the worst and most disastrous day in the whole three hundred and sixty-five. . . . Never were our boasts of liberty so inflated as at this moment, never were they greater mockeries." The reason? This country, said Garrison, was faced with a danger that threatened its very survival—the danger of slavery. This menace, he went on, was so terrible that it should make July 4 a day of fasting and prayer, not one of "boisterous merriment and idle pageantry." He had mounted this platform, he told his listeners, to accuse the entire American people of participation in the crime of slavery, and to plead for

the liberation of two millions of wretched, degraded beings, who are pining in hopeless bondage—over whose sufferings scarcely an eye weeps, or a heart melts, or a tongue pleads either to God or man.

It was not his purpose, Garrison said, to give a lecture on the evils of slavery. He did not intend "to explore even a furlong of that immense wilderness of suffering, which remains unsubdued in our land." No, he took it for granted that his audience understood all this. His purpose was a more practical one: he came to pose a question, and to suggest an answer to it. The question that he posed was this, "What is the duty of Americans with respect to slavery and its abolition?"

To help answer this question Garrison set before his

audience a number of propositions for their consideration.

I assume that the slaves of this country . . . are preeminently entitled to the prayers, and sympathies, and charities of the American people; and that their claims for redress are as strong as those of any Americans could be, in a similar situation.

Garrison here was suggesting something extraordinary and, at that time, quite new. *American slaves,* he was saying, *were American citizens;* and he went on to elaborate this point:

A very large proportion of our colored population were born upon our soil, and are therefore entitled to the privileges of American citizens. This is their country by birth, not by adoption. Their children possess the same inherent and inalienable rights as ours; and it is a crime of the blackest dye to load them with fetters.

It is important for us to understand that what Garrison was saying to his Park Street audience was not only new but also revolutionary in its implications. Until he appeared on the scene, almost no whites in the United States believed that black people were, or had a right to become, full citizens of the United States. Slaves were Africans not Americans, subjects not citizens. Many people, at that time, felt that the best solution to slavery was to ship all the blacks back to Africa. Whites who were worried by the rapid growth of slavery comforted themselves with the thought that there did in fact exist an organization whose aim, precisely, was the colonization and resettlement of the black population. This organization was known as the American Colonization Society, and it had been founded in 1816 to set in motion the work of shipping black people back to Africa, and in particular to Liberia, a West African settlement acquired by the U.S. government in 1822. The Colonization Society sent there such emancipated slaves as chose to go, together with captives liberated by the British or American navies on the high seas.

"Thank God for the Colonization Society," white people thought to themselves. "It is going to rid us of slavery and of black people at one and the same time." But, of course, this was an idle dream. In the forty-four years between its foundation and the Civil War, the Society shipped at most 12,000 ex-slaves to Liberia. At that rate it would have taken several thousand years to have gotten rid of America's total black population and to have resettled it in Africa. To do the job faster would have required an astronomical outlay of funds. Assuming a cost of $1,500 for the purchase, shipment, and settlement of each slave, the sum needed, at a conservative estimate, would have amounted by 1840 to $1.5 trillion. And where, pray, was this money to come from?

Colonizationism, in any event, was the product of a philosophy that we may think of as being both racist and inhuman. It taught that black people must be gotten rid of because their presence in America would contaminate the superior whites; it denied the very idea that these black people who had watered America for two centuries with their blood, sweat, and tears could belong to and inherit, as full citizens, the land on which they had lived and toiled and died.

Garrison's message, therefore, came as a thunderclap

William Lloyd Garrison.

to the Park Street audience and to the American people. These black slaves, he told his fellow citizens, are as good Americans as you are. They possess the same inalienable rights that are set down in the Declaration of Independence as the birthright of all the people who dwell in this land.

Garrison's proposition was revolutionary in another sense. If black people had not yet won the rights to which they were entitled as Americans—why, then, the American Revolution was not yet over! It must go on until all Americans had won the rights of "life, liberty, and the pursuit of happiness" which the Declaration of Independence promised to all. If this revolutionary struggle was not carried through to the end, then the Fourth of July with its firecrackers and rhetoric was a display of hypocrisy unmatched in the history of the human race. "Such a glaring contrast," Garrison pointed out, "as exists between our creed and practice, the annals of six thousand years cannot parallel."

The slaves, said Garrison, in this same proposition, "were entitled to the prayers, and sympathies, and charities of the American people." The statement sounds so harmless that we may easily overlook the hidden thrust of the words. Up until 1829 few white Americans had wasted their prayers or sympathies on slaves. But Garrison simply refused to accept the fact of public indifference to a great national wrong; he was calling for a revolution in public opinion as a result of which the American people would begin to concern themselves with the fate and sufferings of their fellow citizens. Could such a revolution be accomplished? Many in 1829 might have doubted the possibility. But at least one thing was clear: if the majority of Americans ever did challenge the lawfulness and the morality of slavery, the South would encounter a crisis of survival in which the very existence of its peculiar institution would be endangered.

That this was exactly what Garrison had in mind, he made clear in the second proposition he submitted to his Park Street audience, which he stated as follows:

The free states—by which I mean non-slave-holding states—are constitutionally involved in the guilt of slavery, by adhering to a national compact that sanctions it; they have the right to remonstrate against its continuance, and it is their duty to assist in its overthrow.

Garrison here was not advocating violent interference with slavery; such a thing would have been contrary to his nature since he was a pacifist who advocated only the accomplishment of social change by nonviolent means. He foresaw that public opinion, which he thought of as "the lever that can move the moral world," would compel the abolition of slavery by securing constitutional changes. This, he felt, was entirely fair and proper; not only was the abolition of slavery a national interest, but the white population of the North also possessed a decisive majority if ever it should favor this cause. As he pointed out, the population of the free states "is nearly double that of the slave states, and the voice of the overwhelming majority should be potential."

To enter the battle to change the northern mind and to convert the northern soul was, then, in Garrison's view, the principal, the decisive task before antislavery people. "If any man believes," he said,

that slavery can be abolished without a struggle with the

RAFFLE

Mr. Joseph Jennings respectfully informs his friends and the public that, at the request of many acquaintances, he has been induced to purchase from Mr. Osborne, of Missouri, the celebrated

DARK BAY HORSE, "STAR,"

Aged five years, square trotter and warranted sound; with a new light Trotting Buggy and Harness; also, the dark, stout

MULATTO GIRL, "SARAH,"

Aged about twenty years, general house servant, valued at *nine hundred dollars*, and guaranteed, and

Will be Raffled for

At 4 o'clock P. M., February first, at the selection hotel of the subscribers. The above is as represented, and those persons who may wish to engage in the usual practice of raffling, will, I assure them, be perfectly satisfied with their destiny in this affair.

The whole is valued at its just worth, fifteen hundred dollars; fifteen hundred

CHANCES AT ONE DOLLAR EACH.

The Raffle will be conducted by gentlemen selected by the interested subscribers present. Five nights will be allowed to complete the Raffle. BOTH OF THE ABOVE DESCRIBED CAN BE SEEN AT MY STORE, No. 78 Common St., second door from Camp, at from 9 o'clock A. M. to 2 P. M.

Highest throw to take the first choice; the lowest throw the remaining prize, and the fortunate winners will pay twenty dollars each for the refreshments furnished on the occasion.

N. B. No chances recognized unless paid for previous to the commencement.

JOSEPH JENNINGS.

Advertisement for the raffle of
a twenty-year-old slave woman.

worst passions of human nature, quietly, harmoniously,
he cherishes a delusion. . . . Sirs, the prejudices of the
North are stronger than those of the South; they bristle,
like so many bayonets, around the slaves; they forge and
rivet the chains of the nation. Conquer them, and the
victory is won.

Some people might have dismissed Garrison as a mere dreamer, without the power to realize his dreams. How could one poor printer prevail against the mighty spreading empire of the slavery South?

Slaveholders themselves did not dismiss Garrison's words lightly. On the contrary, they reacted with fury and consternation to the challenge that he had flung down; they saw in this antislavery message a spark that could ignite not only the North but the South as well. Nat Turner's rebellion, as we have seen, took place in August 1831, just two years after Garrison gave his historic talk. Could it be, the slaveholders asked themselves, that these words did in fact spark Turner's revolt? They began to see themselves as the defenders of a besieged fortress, facing the assault of a powerful white enemy from outside while at the same time they fought back against an equally powerful black enemy from within.

Garrison's challenge, evidently, must be answered, and his subversive agitation must be put down. The answer was not long in coming. It was drawn up by George McDuffie, governor of South Carolina, and made part of his annual message to the South Carolina Legislature in 1835. Carefully thought out and fashioned, this statement was addressed to the slaveholders and their children, to the northern states, to the American people at large and, finally, to the slaves themselves.

Since your last adjournment [wrote McDuffie], *the public mind, throughout the slaveholding states, has been . . . excited by the wanton, officious, and incendiary proceedings of certain societies and persons of some of the non-slaveholding states, who have been actively employed in attempting to circulate among us, pamphlets, papers, and pictorial representations of the most offensive and inflammatory character, and eminently calculated to seduce our slaves from their fidelity.*

McDuffie was here stating simple fact. Garrison spent two years in Baltimore and then went back to Boston where, in 1831, he launched his newspaper, the *Liberator*, to carry the abolitionist message to the four corners of the country. In 1833 a national organization, the American Antislavery Society, was formed at a convention in Philadelphia, and began to lay plans for a nationwide antislavery campaign. Organizers and agitators began to fan out, carrying the message across the land—in New England, the Central States, the Midwest, and the South.

McDuffie uttered a warning to his listeners. Do not, he said, through contempt or indifference underestimate the danger that this new movement poses for the survival of slavery.

The experience of both Great Britain and France fearfully instruct us, from what small and contemptible beginnings this ami des noirs [friend of the blacks] *philosophy may rise to a gigantic power, too mighty to be resisted by all the influence and energy of the government. . . . It may not unaptly be compared to the element of fire of which a neglected spark, amongst* combustible materials, which a timely stamp of the foot might have extinguished forever, speedily swells into a sweeping torrent of fiery desolation which no human power can arrest or control.

McDuffie again was doing nothing more than reminding his listeners of recent historical facts. In 1789 the French Revolution had broken out, calling for the end of tyranny and the death of tyrants. There was an immediate response in the French sugar island of Haiti, where black slaves under Toussaint L'Ouverture rose up, and, in a fiery ten-year struggle, swept away both slavery and slaveholders. In England the antislavery movement had its first beginnings in the 1780s under the leadership of a tiny band of dedicated abolitionists. Their work led to the abolition of the slave trade in 1809 and of slavery itself in the British West Indies in 1833.

To slaveholder McDuffie, the conclusion to be drawn from these facts was clear enough. People who advocated the abolition of slavery, whether they spoke in South Carolina or any other state, ought to be put to death. "It is my deliberate opinion," as he put it, "that the laws of every community should punish this species of interference by death . . . regarding the authors of it as 'enemies of the human race.' "

But, of course, savage repression of antislavery ideas was, by itself, not enough. Slavery must be defended because it was *right*; it could be defended adequately on no other basis. Slavery, thought McDuffie, must be defended in this way, a basis for it must be found in morality; for without the cooperation of the American people, and to some extent of the slaves themselves, he saw, as clearly as Garrison saw, that slavery could not survive for a single day.

Such a moral defense McDuffie now proceeded to outline. Garrison had attacked slavery for being totally evil; he, McDuffie, would defend it because it was totally good. "No human institution," the governor began,

is more manifestly consistent with the will of God, than domestic slavery, and no one of his ordinances is written in more legible characters than that which consigns the African race to this condition. . . . Whether we consult the sacred Scriptures, or the lights of nature and reason, we shall find these truths as abundantly apparent, as if written with a sunbeam in the heavens. Under both the Jewish and Christian dispensations of our religion, domestic slavery existed with the unequivocal sanction of its prophets, its apostles, and finally its great Author. . . . The patriarchs themselves, those chosen instruments of God, were slave-holders.

With these words McDuffie was outlining what became known as the religious defense of slavery. The ground was well chosen. Millions of Americans thought of the Bible as the word of God, as God's law written down in a book. And where in the Bible could you find any condemnation of slavery?

McDuffie went on to justify slavery on grounds of race. This racist argument asserted that whites were "superior" people, born to rule, and that blacks or other nonwhite people, were "inferior" and born to do the will of whites. The African, said McDuffie, was destined by providence to occupy "a position of servile dependence." This, he said, is marked on the face, stamped on the skin, and evinced by the intellectual inferiority of this race. They have all the qualities that fit them for slaves, and not one of those that would fit them to be freemen. . . . They are in all respects, physical, moral and political, inferior to millions of the human race. . . .

The problem with this racist position was that, apart from its arrogance and falsity, it was hard to use it, by itself, as a justification for slavery. Assume, for the purposes of argument, that Africans were not as smart as everybody else; how did that give you a right to tear them away from their own country and enslave them in a distant land? Didn't a person have an inalienable right to freedom no matter what his intelligence was?

McDuffie anticipated this objection and answered it with an argument that racists have gone on repeating into the twentieth century. Kidnaping Africans and bringing them to the United States had conferred upon these poor dumb black people the greatest of all possible benefits—Christian civilization. "If," he said,

the benevolent friends of the black race would compare the condition of that portion of them which we hold in servitude with that which still remains in Africa, totally unblessed by the lights of civilization or Christianity, and groaning under a savage despotism, as utterly destitute of hope as of happiness, they would be able to form some tolerable estimate, of what our blacks have lost by slavery in America, and what they have gained by freedom in Africa.

Once grant this assumption, that Africans *gain* by being

torn from their homeland and brought to a "civilized" country, and the racist argument may be used with good effect. Since these Africans were inferior and unfit for freedom, argued McDuffie, guardianship must be exercised over them for an indefinite period, and this could be done only by whites. Emancipation and colonization alike were out of the question.

This "guardianship" exercised by whites over blacks, McDuffie went on, was a wise and benevolent one, and it was performed as much in the interest of the slave as in the interest of the master.

It is the obvious interest of the master, not less than his duty, to provide comfortable food and clothing for his slaves . . . the peasantry and operatives of no country in the world are better provided for, in these respects, than the slaves of our country.

People, he went on, had charged that black slaves were overworked, even driven to death. This he denied:

They habitually labor from two to four hours a day less than the operatives in other countries, and it has been truly remarked by some writer, that a Negro cannot be made to injure himself by excessive labor.

The general condition of these happy, carefree people might well be envied by the poverty-stricken peasants and miserable proletarians of other countries! "There is not," he exclaimed, "upon the face of the earth any class of people, high or low, so perfectly free from care and anxiety." Security from the cradle to the grave, this was what slave society had accomplished for its black dependents:

They know that their masters will provide for them, under all circumstances, and that in the extremity of old age, instead of being driven to beggary or to seek public charity in a poor house, they will be comfortably accommodated and kindly treated among their relatives and associates.

Slavery, in a word, was a benevolent and humane social system; it produced feelings of kindness and mutual trust between masters and slaves. Black people in bondage were "cheerful, contented and happy, much beyond the general condition of the human race." Slavery, so far from being evil, was the highest good; it was, indeed, "the cornerstone of the republican edifice."

His defense completed, McDuffie addressed himself to the northern states, and told them bluntly what the South expected of them. All legislative assemblies, he said, were on notice that they must enact "penal laws denouncing the incendiaries of whom we complain, and such punishments as will speedily and forever suppress their machinations against our peace and safety." Do this, he said, or turn over the abolitionists to the South for appropriate punishment.

McDuffie was demanding that American citizens give up their inalienable right to free speech under pain of savage punishment, even death. Would northerners ever agree to such a thing? The speaker added a warning; do this, or face the consequences:

The refusal of a state to punish these offensive proceedings against another, by its citizens or subjects, makes the state so refusing an accomplice in the outrage, and furnishes a just cause of war.

Hangman, Slack on the Line

Hang - man, hang - man, slack on the line,

O father, father, did you bring me money,
    Money to pay my fine?
Or did you come here to see me die
    On this hangman's line?

No, I didn't bring you money,
    Money to pay your fine,
But I just came here to see you die
    Upon this hangman's line.

*repeat sequence with mother, brother, sister,
and lover; the last of these concludes with*

True love, I got gold and silver,
    Money to pay your fine,
How could I bear to see you die
    On this hangman's line?

Reprinted by permission of the publisher from Dorothy Scarborough, *On The Trail of Negro Folk-Songs.* Copyright 1925 by Harvard University Press; 1953 by Mary McDaniel Parker.

DEATH, WITHOUT BENEFIT
OF CLERGY
Elijah Lovejoy, 1833–1837

It is my deliberate opinion that the laws of every community should punish this species of interference by death without benefit of clergy, regarding the authors of it as "enemies of the human race."

George McDuffie, Address to the Legislature of South Carolina, 1835

William Lloyd Garrison launched his antislavery campaign in earnest when he returned to Boston in 1831 and began publication of his newspaper, the *Liberator*. "I am in earnest," he warned his opponents, "I will not equivocate: *and I will be heard.*" People like McDuffie were right to be alarmed; there was no lack of dedicated New Englanders who would listen to Garrison, who would adopt his convictions, and who would spread his word.

A key figure in taking up Garrison's message and carrying it to the Midwest was a theological student named Theodore Weld. Born in 1803, the son of a Hamden, Connecticut, pastor, Weld possessed outstanding organizational ability, personal courage, and a capacity for self-sacrifice. By 1832 Weld had resolved to become a minister, and he had embraced Garrisonian convictions.

Like many young New England ministers of his time, he had a vision of America's future greatness in the settlement of the Mississippi Valley. There, in the Midwest, where one day millions and millions of Americans would live, a man might labor profitably to advance the Christian faith and to convince the people that the abolition of slavery was the highest of Christian duties.

So it was that Weld came to Cincinnati in 1833 and enrolled as a student in Lane Theological Seminary. Lane had been established in 1829 as a center for the training of Presbyterian ministers. Cincinnati was already the leading city of the Midwest, still rapidly growing, and an obvious place to plant an important new college. Cincinnati, as one of Lane's founders wrote, "now at the heart of four millions, and in twenty years to be the heart of twelve millions, is the most important point in our nation for a great central theological institution of the first character." Lane Seminary was located at Walnut Hills, on pleasant wooded highlands, about two miles outside the city, with 125 acres of its own farmland. The college buildings were made of red brick. Immense trees of the primeval forest, beech and oak, shadowed the buildings and provided an impenetrable shade in the summertime. During the fierce gales of autumn and winter the students, as one of them recalled, "used to watch the tossing of the spectral branches and listen to the roaring of the wind through the forest."

Theodore Weld arrived at Lane Seminary in the fall of 1833. When an epidemic of cholera broke out among the students shortly after, Weld at once assumed leadership and organized the care and nursing of the sick. As he got to know his fellow students, many of

Lane Seminary.

whom were from the South, he found that they were hostile to the antislavery cause, or at best indifferent. He began to prepare the ground, accordingly, for a full-scale discussion of the slavery question. A committee was brought together and launched what was probably the first teach-in in American college history.

The Lane teach-in went on for days and days. For eighteen nights in February 1834, the students assembled and debated the slavery question under the leadership of Weld and his committee. Immediatists battled colonizationists. Ought slavery to be abolished, and if so, ought it to be abolished now or later? Were black people American citizens, and ought they to have the rights of citizens? Should they all be shipped back to Africa? Ought the slaveholders to be compensated for the loss of their slaves, or should the slaves be liberated unconditionally?

The final outcome of these long, patient discussions was an overwhelming victory for Garrisonian views. The students then proceeded to organize their own anti-slavery society to make known the abolitionist position, to win converts for it, and to turn it into a reality. Five officers were chosen to direct the Lane Antislavery Society; all of them came from the South.

The reaction of Lane's Board of Trustees to these events was immediate and hysterical. Abolitionism, in those days, was looked upon by most people as the vilest of doctrines, something to be feared even more than cholera itself. An emergency meeting was called, and the student action was denounced in bitter terms. "The spirit of insubordination," as an observer wrote, "resistance to law, and of civil commotion, which they regard the students' action as fostering, was deprecated in a tone to make one shudder." Then the Lane Antislavery Society was abolished by simple decree; and the students were forbidden to say anything or to write anything about antislavery subjects unless they received special permission. New college regulations prohibited

any public meetings or discussions among the students, any public addresses by the students in the Seminary or elsewhere, or appeals or communications to the students at their meals or when assembled on other ordinary occasions, without the approbation of the faculty.

Students who broke these regulations and dared to discuss the slavery question were liable to instant expulsion from the college. As a result, most of the students packed their things and quit. Many of them transferred to nearby Oberlin College. And that, practically speaking, was the end of Lane as a center of learning and Christian enlightenment. It lingered on for twenty years or so, graduating a handful of students every year.

The failure of Lane, of course, did not mark the end of the antislavery movement in the Midwest, but the beginning. Wherever the students went, they took the message with them.

A good example of this is the case of Andrew Benton, who was the recording secretary of the Lane Antislavery Society. Benton left Lane in 1834 and went back to his home town, Saint Louis, Missouri, where he became the "agent" or local organizer for the American Antislavery Society. He soon met a young minister named Elijah Lovejoy and converted him to Garrisonian views. Thus the stage was set for a new and important step in the development of the antislavery struggle.

Elijah Lovejoy, like William Lloyd Garrison and Theodore Weld, was from New England. He was born in 1802 in Waterville, Maine, the son of a Congregational minister. Lovejoy graduated in 1826 from Waterville College at the top of his class, and headed west; the Mississippi Valley, its fertility, beauty and multiplying population, captured his imagination. He would dedicate his life, he resolved, to spreading the word of God among these westerners!

In November 1833, as part of his purpose, and having settled in Saint Louis, Lovejoy issued the first number of a new journal, the *Saint Louis Observer*. Its pages were to be devoted to "Christian politics, diffusion of religious intelligence, and the saving of souls." The *Observer* did not have a long life—the last issue appeared less than four years later, in 1837. But, as we shall see, its impact upon the antislavery movement was to be second only to that of Garrison's *Liberator*.

When the *Observer* began publication, Lovejoy had no particular convictions about slavery, but his discussions with Andrew Benton changed all that; he began to feel, like so many others, the full impact of Garrisonian ideas. So it was that in a little while the *Observer* began to attack slavery as a national sin and as a cruel form of human oppression. Saint Louis was the capital of a slaveholding state, and the community's reaction was predictable. The city's newspapers began to resound with curses against Lovejoy; leading citizens organized and attended mass meetings which demanded that the *Observer* be suppressed. Racist hysteria vented itself upon the black inhabitants of Saint Louis, who were abused and assaulted in the streets. White people were urged to denounce anybody even suspected of holding abolitionist views, and to report them to the authorities.

A weaker man than Lovejoy would have shut up shop and left town; but not he. As a matter of fact he began to speak out even more boldly than before. In April 1836 the steamboat *Flora* docked at Saint Louis, and Frank McIntosh, a black crewman, went ashore. Arrested in a street brawl, he killed one of his captors and was lodged in jail. A mob formed, took him from the jail, chained him to a tree, and burned him to death, heedless of the man's agonizing screams and his pleading for a bullet to end his sufferings.

Next day Lovejoy visited the scene and viewed the charred body. His protest against the atrocity appeared in the *Observer* of May 5 under the heading *Awful Murder and Savage Barbarity*. Nobody was arrested or tried for the murder of Frank McIntosh, but the mob decided to put Lovejoy out of business. His office was wrecked on May 23 and once again in July.

And so Lovejoy was driven out of Saint Louis. With his wife, Celia, and his young son, he fled northward up the Mississippi and located his press on free soil, in the riverside community of Alton, Illinois.

There, at Alton, the struggle broke out again. On July 24, when the press was landed at the wharf, a band of Missourians seized it and threw it into the river. Lovejoy then secured a second press from Cincinnati, installed it, and began once more to publish. Now it was the turn of the Alton townspeople to become enraged at his ideas; in July 1837 a mass meeting was held at the Market House under the leadership of prominent citizens. Lovejoy was ordered to stop the diffusion of "dangerous and inflammatory doctrines." When he refused to abandon his right to publication, a mob invaded the *Observer* office on August 21, tore apart the press, and scattered the type. Lovejoy secured a third press. Once again, when this press arrived just one month later, on September 21, 1837, it was broken up and dumped in the Mississippi.

At this point Lovejoy left Alton and journeyed north some sixty miles to Jacksonville, Illinois, to attend the annual commencement exercises at Illinois College. He sought the help and support of the Presbyterian ministers who assembled at Jacksonville for this occasion. Among them was Edward Beecher, the president of Illinois College. It was the same Edward Beecher who had opened his church in Boston to William Lloyd Garrison on July 4, 1829. Beecher, fired with the same vision of midwestern destiny as had taken hold also of Lovejoy and Weld, had come to Jacksonville the year following Garrison's July 4 address, and had brought his antislavery convictions with him.

Lovejoy and Beecher were both Presbyterian ministers, and by 1837 they had become fast friends. Beecher, who had been watching developments at Alton with close attention, decided that the time had come to intervene. "I had," he wrote, "up to this time not participated at all in the public discussion which was so deeply exciting the nation, but had merely been an attentive and thoughtful spectator." Now he and his colleagues called an Illinois convention to mobilize support for Lovejoy and for the struggle for a free press. This meeting, designed to set up an Illinois antislavery society, would

Edward Beecher.

take place at Alton beginning October 26, 1837.

When the convention met, a rude surprise was in store for Beecher and his friends. Leaders of the local Colonization Society packed the meeting with Lovejoy's enemies, and they proceeded to take over. A report was prepared and submitted recommending that Lovejoy be barred from publishing any newspaper in the city. Said the report,

> While there appears to be no disposition to prevent the liberty of free discussion, through the medium of the press or otherwise, as a general thing, it is deemed a matter indispensable to the peace and harmony of this community, that the labors and influence of the late editor of the Observer be no longer identified with any newspaper establishment in the city.

Such a "compromise," the writers thought, was moderate and fair. It would restore peace and order to the distracted community.

Then Lovejoy rose to speak on his own behalf and to urge the meeting to reject this recommendation. In the presence of his enemies, the editor of the *Observer* delivered perhaps one of the most moving pleas for human rights, that has ever been uttered on American soil. "With a tranquil, self-possessed air," Beecher recalled, "he went up to the bar within which the chairman sat, and in a tone of deep, tender, and subdued feeling, spoke." Lovejoy spoke without notes. As both he and Beecher remembered it later, this is what he said:

> Mr. Chairman, I do not admit that it is the business of this assembly to decide whether I shall or shall not

publish a newspaper in this city. The gentlemen have, as the lawyers say, made a wrong issue. I have the right to do it. I know that I have the right freely to speak and publish my sentiments, subject only to the laws of the land for the abuse of that right. This right was given me by my Maker; and is solemnly guaranteed to me by the Constitution of these United States and of this state.

Then Lovejoy restated the issue as he saw it, bearing in mind that two of his presses had already been destroyed by Alton people without the mayor lifting a finger to prevent or punish the deed; bearing in mind too that, even as he spoke, a boat was on its way with yet another press. "It is" he said, "simply a question whether the law shall be enforced, or whether the mob shall be allowed, as they are now, to continue to trample it under their feet, by violating with impunity the rights of an innocent individual."

If, Lovejoy continued, his friends asked him to give up his post as editor of the *Observer*, that was one thing; but he would not resign his job at the dictate of a mob. In telling the truth as he saw it he was serving the American people. "A voice," he said,

comes to me from Maine, from Massachusetts, from Connecticut, from New York, from Pennsylvania; yea, from Kentucky, from Mississippi, from Missouri; calling upon me in the name of all that is dear in heaven or earth, to stand fast; and by the help of God, I WILL STAND. I know I am but one and you are many. My strength would avail little against you all. You can crush me if you will; but I shall die at my post, for I cannot and will not forsake it.

Lovejoy's audience listened to him, and they must have been amazed. What kind of obstinate folly was this, that a man would die rather than surrender his right to edit an obscure, poorly printed propaganda sheet? Patiently Lovejoy went on to explain. As he listened, Edward Beecher put his head down upon his hands and wept. "Why should I flee from Alton?" Lovejoy asked.

Is not this a free state? When assailed by a mob at St. Louis, I came hither, as to the home of freedom and of the laws. The mob has pursued me here, and why should I retreat again? Where can I be safe if not here? Have I not a right to claim the protection of the laws? What more can I have in any other place? Sir, the very act of retreating will embolden the mob to follow me wherever I go. No, sir: there is no way to escape the mob, but to abandon the path of duty; and that, God helping me, I will never do.

There was a silence. Lovejoy's eyes rested on his listeners. You have declared yourselves my enemies, he said, and your hands are against me, almost every one. What, he said, have I done to deserve this? "I appeal to every individual present: whom of you have I injured? Whose character have I traduced? Whose family have I molested? Whose business have I meddled with? If any, let him here rise and testify against me."

No word spoke the listeners; none rose to answer his challenge, to accuse him of wrongdoing. I am an innocent man, said Lovejoy, and I have committed no crime! But, you, you who listen to me now,

you come together for the purpose of driving out a con-

fessedly innocent man, for no cause but that he dares to think and speak as his conscience and his God dictate. Will conduct like this stand the scrutiny of your country? Of posterity? Above all, of the Judgment Day?

Like many others who suffered persecution before or after his time, Lovejoy pleaded with his audience to defend his right to speak lest their own consciences torment them ever after. "Pause, I beseech you," he urged them. "The present excitement will soon be over; the voice of conscience will at last be heard. And in some season of honest thought, even in this world, as you review the scenes of this hour, you will be compelled to say, *he was right, he was right.*"

Lovejoy had been urged to leave Alton "quietly," like a gentleman, not to disgrace himself or the community by making a fuss. He rejected this advice with contemptuous defiance. "You cannot disgrace me," he exclaimed.

You may burn me at the stake, as they did McIntosh at St. Louis; or you may tar and feather me, or throw me into the Mississippi, as you have often threatened to do; but you cannot disgrace me. I, and I alone, can disgrace myself; and the deepest of all disgrace would be, at a time like this to deny my Master by forsaking his cause. He died for me: and I were most unworthy to bear his name, should I refuse, if need be, to die for him.

Now Lovejoy came to the hardest part. They had, before the meeting, taken him aside privately and reasoned with him. "If you do not fear for yourself," they had told him, "at least show some consideration for your family. You have a wife and small son who are dependent upon you, who need you." "It is true, Mr. Chairman," he said, and the tears glistened in his eyes,

I am a husband and father; and this it is that adds the bitterest ingredient to the cup of sorrow I am called to drink. I am made to feel the wisdom of the Apostle's advice, "it is better not to marry." . . . How was it the other night, on my return to the house? I found my wife driven to the garret, through fear of the mob, who were prowling around the house. And scarcely had I entered ere my windows were broken in by the brickbats of the mob; and she so alarmed that it was impossible for her to sleep or rest that night.

Then, from the throat of this gentle man, a cry as agonized as any cry raised by a fugitive slave. "I am hunted," he cried, "as a partridge upon the mountains. I am pursued as a felon through your streets; and to the guardian power of the law I look in vain for that protection against violence which even the vilest criminal may claim."

Lovejoy sat down, the discussion became general. Speaker after speaker attacked him as a fanatic, a madman. A vote of censure was submitted and adopted by acclamation. "We regret," it said, "that persons and editors from abroad have seen proper to interest themselves so conspicuously in the discussion and agitation of a question, in which our city is made the principal theater."

Thus the meeting ended. The crisis was at hand. Remember that Lovejoy's third press had been destroyed by the mob on September 21, 1837. He had made arrangements to have a fourth press sent in from the East.

This press now arrived from Saint Louis by boat on November 6. The antislavery party, headed by Beecher and Lovejoy, unloaded it in the early hours of November 7 and lodged it on the third floor of Godfrey and Gilman's warehouse. The group, numbering about thirty in all, were divided into watches of six men to guard the warehouse on successive nights.

This job, in the few hours that remained until dawn on November 7, fell to Lovejoy and Beecher. "The morning soon began to dawn," wrote Beecher,

and that morning I shall never forget. Who that has stood on the banks of the mighty stream that then rolled before me can forget the emotions of sublimity that filled his heart, as in imagination he has traced those channels of intercourse opened by it and its branches through the illimitable regions of this Western world? I thought of future ages, and of the countless millions that should dwell on this mighty stream; and that nothing but the truth would make them free.

That morning Beecher said good-bye to his friend and returned to Jacksonville. The worst, he thought, was over. The press had been successfully landed in the dead of night, while the mob slept. It was safe in the warehouse under guard. Soon it would be taken up to Lovejoy's office, and the *Observer* would resume publication.

That night the mob attacked. There was an exchange of fire between attackers and defenders. Lyman Bishop, one of the attackers, was killed. Others set up a ladder, mounted to the roof of the building, and set it on fire. Lovejoy and his friends came out, fired their guns, dispersed the attackers, and went back to reload. On com-

Riot at Alton, November 7, 1837.

ing out for a second time, Lovejoy was hit by five bullets and killed. The rest of the defenders fled the burning warehouse, being fired upon as they went. The mob entered the warehouse and destroyed Lovejoy's fourth and final press.

When the news of Lovejoy's death reached Edward Beecher, he sat down, penned his account of the tragedy, and published it as a little pamphlet entitled *Narrative of Riots at Alton in Connection with the Death of Rev. Elijah P. Lovejoy.* It was addressed to a nation deeply torn and troubled by the news. Some rejoiced, with McDuffie, that antislavery agitators were put to death. And others asked themselves this question: *Who are these slaveholders, that they should tell us what we may or may not discuss?*

As for Beecher's little book, it was read and reread in antislavery circles. It told the story of the martyrdom of a Christian patriot, and it explained the meaning of that martyrdom.

Was Lovejoy, Beecher asked, an instrument of sedition and of social disturbance, as his enemies charged? Was he a malicious troublemaker? No, said Beecher. He was a Christian leader tackling one of the fundamental problems of the age, the problem of slavery. In doing this he was an instrument for the expression of God's will. God's plan, in the nineteenth century of the Christian era, was for the abolition of slavery throughout the world.

God's will, wrote Beecher, must be heeded and obeyed. Americans, like anybody else, must listen to the voice of God or suffer the consequences. Edward Beecher envisioned the Midwest as the home of a free and mighty people who had purged themselves of the sin of slavery and racism. This vision could be made a reality only when men and women had the right to speak the truth and to make it known. *Free speech*, said Beecher, *free inquiry, these are God's chosen instruments for the renovation of the world.*

And those who suppress the truth, who take up fire and sword and suppress the truth, who are they? They are the enemies of God. Lovejoy's martyrdom, wrote Beecher, was a warning, and America must heed that warning if it was to be saved. We have, said he,

intelligence and conscience, and religion enough to save our nation, if they can be brought into action with united power. And I confide in God that it will at last be done; that one warning so dreadful will be enough, and that by timely repentance we shall escape the impending judgments of God.

By 1838 the white midwestern minister, Beecher, had come to the same conclusion as the southern black prophet, Turner. *Only action against slavery could save this nation from doom.* Tremendous conclusion! Free whites, as well as black slaves, were now beginning to take action against slavery.

UNREASONABLE SEIZURES
Fair Trial for Fugitives, 1842

The right of the people to be secure in their persons, houses, papers, and effects against unreasonable searches and seizures, shall not be violated, and no warrants shall issue but upon probable cause, supported by oath or affirmation, and particularly describing the place to be searched, and the persons or things to be seized.

Bill of Rights, Article IV

How, in 1837, did most northern people stand in relation to the developing battle between slaveholders and abolitionists? As far as their mental attitude was concerned, northern whites, generally speaking, had a good deal in common with the slaveholders. If you had taken a poll at that time, you would have found that a majority of northerners shared George McDuffie's view that blacks were lazy, inferior people to be despised, used, and feared all at the same time. To the extent that they thought about the matter at all many northerners were colonizationists. Blacks, they would have felt, ought not be allowed to hang around to pollute the white man's land. Ship 'em back to Africa, where they came from.

When Garrison and the abolitionists began to demand full citizenship as well as freedom for blacks, it didn't just shock southerners, it shocked the whole country. Northern writers, ministers, and politicians joined Mc-Duffie in hysterical denunciation; the public went along with it, at least at first. Sure, they thought, abolitionists are mad dogs and ought to be in jail. Even, maybe, if like Lovejoy they got themselves killed, it wasn't so bad. Like McDuffie said, they were wild men who deserved "death without benefit of clergy."

Therefore, when the antislavery movement got launched during the 1830s it had a rough time. Violence didn't always end in death, as with Lovejoy, but violence was not unusual. Garrison himself was almost lynched by a well-dressed Boston mob in 1836, and came near to losing his life. Theodore Weld and other traveling antislavery organizers were met wherever they went by jeering, rock-throwing crowds. Amos Dresser, a Lane student who took the antislavery message into the South, was publicly flogged for his pains. James G. Birney, an Alabama slaveholder converted by Weld to abolitionism, found the South too hot to hold him. He fled to Cincinnati in 1835 and began to publish an antislavery sheet, the *Philanthropist*. His press shared the fate of Lovejoy's when the mob threw it into the Ohio River, July 30, 1836.

Northern whites, in truth, had no love for blacks, did not particularly like the idea of their either being in America or staying here, and were certainly not in favor of their enjoying the same political rights as others. Thousands of black people lived in the poverty-stricken ghettoes of northern cities; Philadelphia, New York, Boston, and Cincinnati all had black ghettoes. The black people who lived there were referred to as "inhabitants" rather than "citizens." These "inhabitants" in most states were denied many rights to which white people were entitled—for example, voting or sitting on juries. In most northern states, too, blacks were forbidden by law from intermarrying with whites, from going to the same schools, from riding in the same buses or railroad coaches.

The attitude of the average northern white man to black people was expressed to perfection by Abraham Lincoln in a campaign speech that he made in Charleston, Illinois, in 1858:

> I am not, nor have I ever been, in favor of bringing about in any way the social and political equality of the white and black races . . . I am not, nor ever have been, in favor of making voters of the free Negroes, or jurors, or qualifying them to hold office, or having them marry with white people. I will say, in addition, that there is a physical difference between the white and black races which, I suppose, will forever forbid the two races living together upon terms of social and political equality; and inasmuch as they cannot so live . . . while they do remain together . . . I, as much as any other man, am in favor of the superior position being assigned to the white man.

It is, therefore, strange and fascinating to record that northern whites, in spite of their general sympathy with the slaveholder, began, gradually and timidly at first, to take action *against* him. The whites, sure enough, were bitterly prejudiced against black people. *But it did not follow that, because they rejected northern black people as brothers and sisters, as equals, that they believed*

that such northern black people ought to be enslaved.
Northerners joined with the abolitionists, first of all, to
protect *northern* black people, *free* black people like
Solomon Northup, from being kidnaped and enslaved.
This tiny "innocent" question brought them headlong,
as we shall see, into conflict with the empire of slavery
itself.

To spell out the procedures necessary to put Article
IV, clause 2, into effect, Congress passed in 1793 a law
that has become known as "the fugitive felon and slave
law." Section 3 of this law laid down the procedure to
be followed in the extradition of black runaways, that is,
in securing their return from the state to which they
fled to the state of origin. Power was given to the slaveholder or his agent *himself* to arrest a black fugitive, in
the following words:

> *When a person held to labor in any of the United
> States under the laws thereof, shall escape into any other
> of the said states or territories, the person to whom such
> service or labor is due, his agent or attorney, is hereby
> empowered to seize or arrest such fugitive from labor.*

Ordinarily, American law requires that if a person is
to be arrested and charged with a crime, an arrest warrant must first be issued. This is an order in writing,
directed to the police, and signed by a magistrate, au-
thorizing the arrest of a designated person. Normally a
magistrate will not issue such a warrant unless he has
first received information from a citizen or an officer of
the law about the commission of a crime; and unless
he is satisfied that there are sufficient grounds to believe

that a crime has actually been committed. But under section 3 of the "fugitive slave law" these well-established procedures were simply brushed aside. The slave owner or his agent was given the power to track down his quarry and seize the slave wherever he sought refuge—in a private house, a barn, or a haystack.

What, after this, was the next step? How, under the law, was the master supposed to "prove title," and secure permission to take the person he had seized back with him to his native state?

The Act of 1793 gave only a vague answer to such questions. The owner or agent was "empowered" to take the fugitive before either a federal judge or a local magistrate, and to submit proof of ownership either orally or in written form. The court, if satisfied, was then obliged to issue a certificate of ownership. Armed with this legal paper, the slaveholder might then remove the fugitive and take him back south.

In practice, slaveholders often ignored this provision of the law. They felt that they had a right to seize a fugitive without any formality at all, as casually as they might have repossessed a stray calf or a wandering child. When certificates *were* issued, they would read as follows:

Whereas John a negro man about twenty-seven years of age of black complexion has been claimed before me, Jonathan T. Knight, an Associate judge of the Court of Common Pleas of Philadelphia County by Richard Ireland Jones of Anne Arundel County, Maryland, as a fugitive from service . . . and I being satisfied upon proof made to my satisfaction that the said John does owe *labor and service to the said Richard Ireland Jones under the laws of Maryland . . . I have granted to the said Richard Ireland Jones this certificate, which shall be sufficient warrant to him . . . for removing the said John.*

In the opening years of the nineteenth century, black fugitives by the hundreds were crossing the Pennsylvania border from Maryland each year. Maryland began to press Pennsylvania to cooperate more fully than she had been in capturing these runaways and securing their return. Pennsylvania responded by passing an act that made it harder than ever for the Marylanders to get their slaves back. This Pennsylvania Act of 1826 soon became famous. It was entitled "An Act to give effect to the provisions of the Constitution of the United States relative to fugitives from labor, for the protection of free people of color, and to prevent kidnapping."

It was the "protection of free people of color," and the prevention of the kidnaping of free black people that was the main thing in the minds of the Pennsylvania Legislature when it passed the Act of 1826. The right of slave owners under the federal law to seize black people without a warrant—was this not, they asked themselves, in effect an authorization to slaveholders to seize any black person they pleased, whether that person was a slave or not? And did not such an authorization put *all* free black people in Pennsylvania in continued and mortal danger?

The Pennsylvania Act of 1826 provided that the kidnaping of free black people, and their sale or removal from the state, was a crime punishable by fine and imprisonment. The act put an end to private arrest of fugitives by requiring that such people could be arrested

Hunting fugitives.

only by Pennsylvania law officers, and only after the issue of a proper warrant. The act made it harder for slave owners to "prove title." Henceforth, no arrest warrant was to be issued unless the owner first of all submitted a written statement giving the name, age, and general description of the fugitive he sought.

The Act of 1826 had shortcomings which the anti-slavery lawyers grumbled about. If a black person was seized and taken before a judge, the slave owner would say: "Your Honor, this man is my slave, who ran away from me, and whom I have found hiding in the Lancaster County woods." Such an accusation was a very serious one. It was a *criminal* charge, because if a man was found "guilty" of being a slave, terrible punishment followed: loss of all civil and human rights, probably severe physical punishment as well, and, finally, loss of freedom for life. Should not *any* person, asked lawyers, exposed to so terrible an accusation, have the right to defend himself? Should he not enjoy the right to a fair and impartial trial—the right, that is, to summon witnesses for his defense, the right to employ skilled legal counsel, the right to trial before a jury of people chosen from the neighborhood in which the alleged runaway was picked up?

The Act of 1793 did not guarantee these rights to accused fugitives, and the Pennsylvania Act of 1826 did not remedy the terrible deficiency. But it was nonetheless a pioneer measure in the history of the civil rights movement. In the years that followed, other northern states used the Pennsylvania law as a model for laws of their own—and added their own improvements. New York's Act of 1840, to which Solomon Northup owed his freedom, laid upon the governor of the state the obligation to see that kidnaped New Yorkers were "restored to liberty and returned to this State." All expenses incurred in rescuing kidnap victims were to be paid out of the state treasury. The Vermont Act of 1840 granted the right to a jury trial to fugitives, and provided that the costs of defense, if necessary, be borne by the state.

These rights of accused persons—the right to legal not arbitrary arrest, the right to a fair trial, the right to counsel—are guaranteed by the Fourth, Fifth, and Sixth Amendments to the federal Constitution. But in practice, when it came to capturing and dragging back fugitives, these provisions of the Constitution were simply ignored. The Pennsylvania Act of 1826, and the other state laws that soon followed, were important because they declared that the Bill of Rights did exist, and that it must be used to defend black people as well as whites. State laws which insisted that black people, as much as whites, were entitled to "due process of law," were called "liberty laws."

Liberty laws such as the Pennsylvania Act of 1826 or the Vermont Act of 1840 had a twofold impact on the recovery of fugitives. Liberty laws, in the first place, increased the danger involved in hunting slaves and catching them. A white man might hate abolitionists, and he might go along with all the antiblack laws on the books, but he still might react with fury to the sight of a human being being dragged away from free soil into bondage. The tide of antislavery feeling in the United States began to rise with Garrison's July 4 address in 1829, and it went on rising until the outbreak of the Civil War. As the tide rose, so rose the hatred of the people for slave owners and the danger, accordingly, of physical violence and obstruction to which the agents of slavery operating in the northern states were exposed.

Liberty laws, in the second place, threatened to make of the entire North a haven for fugitives and a passageway to Canada. This situation threatened much more than individual property rights. Liberty laws symbolized the opposition of an entire people to the empire of slavery.

As the 1830s wore on, the operation of the liberty laws made it harder and harder to catch slaves in the North. At the same time, southerners became more determined than ever to assert their constitutional right to retrieve their runaway property.

The North claimed that black people accused of being fugitives were entitled, as much as slaveholders were, to enjoy constitutional rights, and they dared to pass state laws to prove it. Very well! Let the Supreme Court decide who had the greater right: the slaveholders or the blacks. Acting on behalf of Maryland slaveholders, the state of Maryland arranged with the state of Pennsylvania in 1841 to submit this issue to the Supreme Court of the United States for arbitration. The questions posed to the Court were these: Was the Pennsylvania Act of 1826 constitutional or not? Did it defeat the slaveholder's right to the extradition of black fugitives? Were the states entitled to pass civil rights laws protecting the rights of blacks that might render extradition more difficult, dangerous, or uncertain?

The case that was chosen to test these issues was *Prigg v. Pennsylvania*. It arose in the following way.

Margaret Morgan was a Maryland slave, the property of a Mrs. Ashmore. In 1832, Margaret Morgan escaped with her child and fled north to Philadelphia. There she lived for five years; another child was born to her.

In 1837, Edward Prigg, who was Mrs. Ashmore's agent, tracked down Margaret Morgan, had her arrested, and brought her before a magistrate. This magistrate refused to hear the case—evidently he wanted no part of the business of sending people back to slavery. Under the Pennsylvania Act of 1826, Prigg ought to have applied to another court for a hearing and a certificate of ownership. Prigg, like many slave catchers before him, preferred to short-circuit the formalities. He simply took Margaret Morgan and her children back to Maryland without asking anyone's permission. There had been no hearing, no "proving of title," no issuance of a certificate of ownership.

Prigg then returned to Pennsylvania and was arrested and indicted in York County for the felony of kidnaping Margaret Morgan, that is, for carrying out the removal of a black person from Pennsylvania without the authorization of the state. Under the Act of 1826 such unauthorized removal was declared a felony, or serious crime: "If any person," said the Act,

shall by force and violence take and carry away any negro from any part of this commonwealth, to any other place, out of this commonwealth with a design of selling or of keeping as a slave for life, every such person on conviction thereof, shall be deemed guilty of a felony.

Prigg was found guilty and the sentence was affirmed

by the state supreme court. The conviction was at once appealed to the U.S. Supreme Court on the grounds that the Pennsylvania Act of 1826 was unconstitutional and the conviction, therefore, void.

The nine-man Court was composed of five southerners and four northerners. It struck down the Pennsylvania Act of 1826. Edward Prigg was, therefore, not guilty of kidnaping Margaret Morgan.

Why did the Court believe that the state of Pennsylvania had acted beyond its lawful powers? The right of slaveholders to recover their slaves, said the Court, was "a positive unqualified right" which no state law might restrain or control. This right of recovery was, in other words, a *national* right, and slaveholders possessed it unconditionally; it was immune to definition, limitation, or regulation by state law. Slaveholders' claims, furthermore, must be met without delay which would cheat the owners of the labor power to which they were legally entitled. Joseph Story of Connecticut handed down the Court's opinion. "Any state law," said Mr. Justice Story, "that limits, delays or postpones the right of the owner to the immediate possession of the slave, and the immediate command of his service and labor, operates to that extent as a discharge of the slave therefrom."

Story stated his conclusion in sweeping language. The right of recapture, he said,

is an absolute positive right and duty, pervading the whole Union with an equal and supreme force, uncontrolled and uncontrollable by any state sovereignty or state legislation. The right of recapture is a new and positive right . . . confined to no territorial limits and bounded by no state institutions or policy.

The power to enforce the slaveholder's right to recapture his runaways, thought Story, rested exclusively with the federal government; the states must adopt a hands-off policy. They were not entitled to interfere in any way.

What about the Fourth, Fifth, and Sixth Amendments to the Constitution—about the rights, that is, of a person to due process of law when exposed to a criminal accusation? Joseph Story simply ignored them. He believed, as Justice Taney would later spell out in Dred Scott's case, that the federal Bill of Rights was *for whites only*; it wasn't designed to protect black people. Story was coming very close indeed to arguing that slaveholders were above the law; that is, slaveholders, in getting what belonged to them, did not have to be bound by the rule of law that applied to everybody else.

The reaction of the northern states to the Prigg decision was predictable. Recapturing runaways was the job of the federal government? All right, said the states, let them do it all by themselves, we will have no part of it. One after another northern states passed laws forbidding state officials from helping the federal government in any way to enforce the fugitive slave law. The *Prigg* decision was handed down in January 1842. Vermont passed "an Act for the Protection of Personal Liberty" in 1843. "No sheriff, deputy sheriff, high sheriff, constable, jailer or other officer or citizen of this state," said section 2 of the law,

shall, hereafter, seize, arrest, or detain, or aid in the seizure, arrest or detention, or imprisonment in any jail or other building, belonging to this state, or to any county, town, city or person therein, of any person for the reason that he is or may be claimed a fugitive slave.

The first wave of liberty laws, starting with the Pennsylvania Act of 1826, upheld the due process rights of black fugitives. The second wave of liberty laws, passed by the states *after* the *Prigg* decision was handed down, defied the power of the slaveholders and called upon the people to resist the enforcement, in their own communities, of a slaveholder's law. The result of this was that it became difficult, and in some cases impossible, to catch runaways in northern states by the time the Mexican War broke out in 1846.

By that time, a lot of people in the North were using an old-fashioned word for the claim that slave catchers were above the law. It was the same word that the Americans had used against the British after the Boston Tea Party. They called it *tyranny*.

Michael Row the Boat Ashore

Michael's boat's a gospel boat,
Halleluja,
Michael's boat's a gospel boat,
Halleluja.

Trumpet sound the jubilee,
Halleluja,
Trumpet sound the jubilee,
Halleluja.

Trumpet sound for rich and poor,
Halleluja,
Trumpet sound for rich and poor,
Halleluja.

Trumpet sound the world around,
Halleluja,
Trumpet sound the world around,
Halleluja.

Trumpet sound for you and me,
Halleluja,
Trumpet sound for you and me,
Halleluja.

Michael row the boat ashore,
Halleluja,
Michael row the boat ashore,
Halleluja.

Jordan's river is chilly and wide,
Halleluja,
Milk and honey on the other side,
Halleluja.

Jordan's river is chilly and cold,
Halleluja,
Chills the body but not the soul,
Halleluja.

RULE OR RUIN
John C. Calhoun's Advice to Slaveholders, 1850

Your purpose, plainly stated, is that you will destroy the government, unless you be allowed to construe and force the Constitution as you please, on all points in dispute between you and us. You will rule or ruin in all events.

Abraham Lincoln, The Cooper Institute Address, February 27, 1860

July 4, 1845, was celebrated across the Union with the usual speeches, processions, fireworks, and parades. Southerners, and slaveholders in particular, had an extra cause for rejoicing. On that day Texas was admitted to the Union as a slave state.

The admission of Texas in this way also guaranteed war with Mexico, for Texas was a Mexican province that declared its independence from Mexico in 1836, an act that the Mexican government had never recognized.

The war began, like most nineteenth-century wars, with fine enthusiasm. Volunteers flocked to the colors, glad of the chance for a free trip to Mexico to teach the Mexicans a lesson. In May 1846, General Zachary Taylor launched his northern invasion of Mexico, crossed the Rio Grande, and took possession of Matamoros. Military encampments sprang up along the river northward toward Camargo. The men began to die like flies from fever and disease.

As the news trickled back home, northerners began to have second thoughts about the morality of a war whose purpose was to extend slavery to territory where it had not existed before. In July 1846, Henry David Thoreau went to jail in Concord, Massachusetts, in protest against the war. "Americans," he wrote in his famous essay, "Civil Disobedience," "must cease to hold slaves and to make war on Mexico, though it cost them their existence as a people."

The next month, August, Congress was in session to debate and act on President Polk's demand for $3 million. The purpose of this money, according to the President, was to make negotiations with Mexico easier by enabling him to purchase Mexican territory. David Wilmot, a lawyer from Pennsylvania, rose to offer an amendment to the bill,

that, as an express and fundamental condition to the *acquisition of any territory from the republic of Mexico by the United States . . . neither slavery nor involuntary servitude shall ever exist in any part of said territory. . . ."*

Wilmot's Proviso, as it was called, passed the House and was turned down in the Senate. But it provided a political program around which northern opposition to slavery could rally. The proviso did not oppose expansion, the winning of new territory by purchase or conquest. It simply said that territorial expansion must not be accompanied by slavery. Ten northern

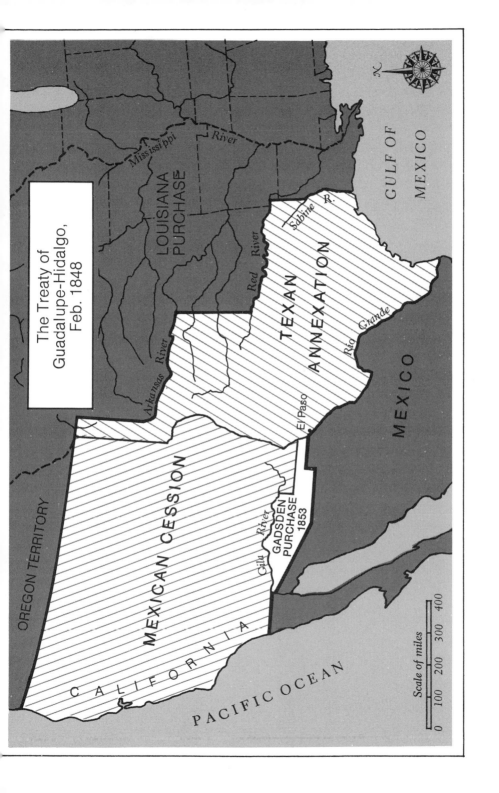

The Treaty of Guadalupe-Hidalgo, Feb. 1848

LOUISIANA PURCHASE

TEXAN ANNEXATION

MEXICAN CESSION

GADSDEN PURCHASE 1853

CALIFORNIA

OREGON TERRITORY

MEXICO

GULF OF MEXICO

PACIFIC OCEAN

Mississippi River

Red River

Arkansas River

Sabine R.

Rio Grande

El Paso

Gila River

Scale of miles
0   100   200   300   400

legislatures passed resolutions endorsing the proviso. The slaveholders read this, rightly, as a fresh challenge to the slavery system and its control of the federal government; one, further, that arose out of a growing awareness among large numbers of northern people of the menace to them of slavery and its constant expansion.

In March 1847, General Winfield Scott launched a second invasion of Mexico through Vera Cruz; by mid-summer he was at the gates of Mexico City. All of Mexico lay before the conqueror. Peace was dictated to the Mexicans and signed at the village of Guadalupe-Hidalgo in February 1848. Mexico surrendered Texas, the incomparable province of California, and the thousand miles of mountain and desert that lay in between.

What was to be done with this vast empire of land that had been won by war and conquest? It was 1848, the year for a presidential election. The Democratic party, which had enjoyed pretty much a monopoly on power in Washington since 1828, nominated Lewis Cass, an aging war hero of 1812 vintage. The opposition party at that time was known as Whig. The Whig party came into existence in 1836; it brought together various groups who were upset by the policies of the Democrats under Andrew Jackson and Martin Van Buren, and who wished to oppose them. To run against Lewis Cass the Whigs nominated a war hero of their own, Zachary Taylor, hero of Matamoros and the Mexican War.

Both the Democratic and Whig parties were national parties; that is, they drew support from people both in the North and the South. The expansion of slavery into new lands won from Mexico was an explosive question which, if it became a major issue in the campaign, threatened to blow both parties apart. Both, therefore, did their best to squelch the issue during the elections. They preferred to concentrate on the safer question of the personalities and records of their respective candidates.

An interesting feature of the 1848 election was the appearance of the Free Soil party which ran former president Martin Van Buren on a Wilmot Proviso platform—no slavery to be permitted in any territories added to the United States by purchase or conquest. The Free Soil party brought together antislavery Democrats into a coalition with abolitionists under their leader James G. Birney. This coalition would provide the nucleus around which another and even greater party, the Republican party, would be organized in 1854.

The question about slavery in the new territories could be postponed for a little while, but not for long. Gold was discovered in California in January 1848; seekers after gold flocked there from the four corners of the globe. In November 1849, the Californians adopted a state constitution banning slavery and demanded admission to the Union. The free-state people already possessed a majority in the federal House of Representatives; with California and other free states soon to follow, free states would hold a majority in the U.S. Senate as well. What, slaveholders began to ask themselves, did this mean for the future of the South and for the survival of slavery?

Such were the circumstances under which Congress reassembled in December 1849. The first point on its agenda was the future of California and the other lands won from Mexico.

In January 1850, Henry Clay of Kentucky set forth a

series of proposals designed to help the North and South to settle their differences. These proposals were the basis for the compromise, or sectional treaty, that was actually passed through Congress later the same year. Clay suggested that California be admitted as a free state, that the New Mexico lands be opened to slave settlers, that slave trading be ended in the District of Columbia, and that a new fugitive slave act be passed to supplement and guarantee the enforcement of the Act of 1793.

On March 4, 1850, a crowded and hushed Senate assembled to hear John C. Calhoun give his answer to Henry Clay. Calhoun was sixty-eight years old at this time, and he was dying. Calhoun, a senator from South Carolina, had married a plantation heiress and was identified both in his personal and political life with the interests and the outlook of the masters of the South. He had long been a southern spokesman and theoretician of the first rank.

Sitting in his room in Hill's boarding house in Washington, D.C., Calhoun had given careful thought about what he was going to say on this, his farewell appearance in the Senate. The advice that he had decided to offer to the South was simple and direct: Secede from the Union, break it up. You can no longer hope to control it, and if others control it, they will use it to accomplish your destruction. He was, in effect, going to advise his friends to draw the sword and to decide by war who should control the United States, its territories, and its government.

Calhoun dictated his speech to Joseph Scoville, his secretary, then made careful corrections in his own hand. March 4 was a bright spring day. Calhoun walked into

John C. Calhoun.

the Senate chamber leaning on the arm of a friend. His form, little more than skin and bones, was draped in a long black cloak. Dark eyes stared from the hollows of the white, emaciated face. He resembled, as one observer put it, "a fugitive from the grave." He handed the manuscript to Senator James Mason of Virginia and sank into his chair. Mason began slowly to read.

Calhoun lost not a moment in coming to the point. "I have, Senators, believed from the first that the agitation of the subject of slavery would, if not prevented by some timely and effective measure, end in disunion." Both major parties, Democrat and Whig, had been deaf to his pleas that steps be taken to prevent this disaster. And the result?

The agitation has been permitted to proceed, with almost no attempt to resist it, until it has reached a period when it can no longer be denied or disguised, that the Union is in danger.

The question, now forced upon Congress, was the ultimate one: How can the Union be preserved?

To answer this question, Calhoun thought it necessary to look at the reasons for southern dissatisfaction with the Union, because it was quite clear to him that, if indeed the Union broke up, it would be because southerners took the initiative. Here he saw two factors that had to be considered. There was this "ceaseless agitation" of the slavery question, which, as George McDuffie had warned fifteen years before, would surely lead to disaster if not checked. But beyond that, Calhoun saw another and to him even more basic factor operating to produce the crisis of the Union. This was the destruction of what he called "sectional equilibrium."

Calhoun went on to explain in detail what he meant by this concept of sectional equilibrium. When, he explained, the Constitution was first set up, the two sections, North and South, were approximately equal in strength. In 1790, when the first census was taken, the total population of the country was 4 million—2 million in the North and 2 in the South; and there were 16 states —8 slave and 8 free. This equality, as measured roughly by population and states, was reflected in the political balance of power that prevailed within the structure of the federal government. In the Senate the slave bloc had sixteen votes, and the free-state bloc, sixteen. In the House of Representatives each bloc had approximately the same number of representatives.

Thus, sectional equilibrium prevailed. Each side balanced the other on the political scales. Neither side possessed in Congress a superiority of votes and, therefore, of political punch with which it could dominate and enforce its will upon the other side.

But, Calhoun went on, with the passage of time, this sectional equilibrium was upset, and the balance of power tilted drastically in favor of the North. He cited the situation revealed by the most recent census, the census of 1840. In this year,

The aggregate population of the United States amounted to 17,063,357, of which the Northern section contained 9,728,920, and the Southern 7,334,437, making a difference, in round numbers, of 2,400,000. The number of states had increased from sixteen to twenty-six, making an addition of ten states. . . . Considering Delaware neutral, the Northern states will have thirteen and the

Southern states twelve, making in the Senate a difference of two Senators in favor of the former. According to the apportionment under the Census of 1840, there were two hundred and twenty-three members in the House of Representatives, of which the Northern states had one hundred and thirty-five, and the Southern states (considering Delaware as neutral) eighty-seven, making a difference in favor of the former in the House of Representatives of forty-eight.

Calhoun then stated his conclusion:

> The result of the whole is to give the Northern section a predominance in every department of the government, and thus concentrate in it the two elements which constitute the Federal government—majority of states, and a majority of their population. . . . Whatever section concentrates the two in itself, possesses the control of the entire government.

This northern superiority that had upset the sectional equilibrium was, *so long as the Union continued,* permanent and irreversible. That very year, 1850, was also a census year. It would show a continued growth of northern population relative to southern; more free states would soon be admitted to the Union. But there were no more slave states to be admitted, because the free-state majority had barred the expansion of slavery to the territories. Yes, the sectional equilibrium had been destroyed; the passage of time would not make the situation better, only worse.

What was the explanation for this dramatic situation where, in the race for land, population, economic development, and political power, the South found itself lagging far behind? Some people might argue that slavery itself had been the great retarding factor, operating as a mighty drag upon the growth of the South. Calhoun, of course, would not have agreed with such an analysis. But, whatever the *reasons* for the sectional disequilibrium, the *fact* was clear enough and not to be disputed: "The North," he said, "has acquired a decided ascendancy over every department of this government, and through it a control over all the powers of the system."

True enough, up to 1850 the North had not chosen to *exercise* its growing powers in a manner that conflicted with the basic interests of the slave-owning South. But Calhoun and the slaveholders had to look to the future. What, in terms of the future, asked Calhoun, were the implications of a superiority of power concentrated in the hands of the free states? As a political realist, he stated the matter exactly as he saw it:

As the North has the absolute control over the government, it is manifest that on all questions between it and the South, where there is a diversity of interests, the interest of the latter will be sacrificed to the former.

Well, he said, this would not be so very important if there were no basic conflict between the sections. *But such was not the case.* There was a vital issue dividing the sections—slavery. "Every portion of the North," he said, "entertains views and feelings more or less hostile to it."

This hostility, Calhoun continued, had long lain dormant, but by 1850 it was a consuming flame fanned to a blaze by the organized antislavery movement. This movement had grown rapidly since its first beginnings in the early 1830s. Then,

for the first time, societies were organized, presses established, lecturers sent forth to excite the people of the North, and incendiary publications scattered over the whole South through the mail. The South was thoroughly aroused. Meetings were held everywhere, and resolutions adopted, calling upon the North to arrest the threatened evil.

This agitation, Calhoun went on, had begun small, but by 1850 it had assumed the dimensions of a mass movement, to the point that it now endangered the Union itself.

With the success of their first movement, this small fanatical party began to acquire strength; and with that, to become an object of courtship of both of the great parties. . . . The infection has extended over both, and the great mass of the population of the North who, whatever may be their opinion of the original abolition party, . . . hardly ever fail, when it comes to acting, to cooperate in carrying out their measures.

Calhoun traced the steady growth of antislavery opinion in the 1840s. Following the *Prigg* decision, there developed a mass movement of opposition to the return of fugitives. Abolitionists were able

to induce the legislatures of most of the Northern states to pass acts which, in effect, threatened to abrogate the clause of the Constitution that provides for the delivering up of fugitive slaves.

The protest movement had gone from success to success. Following David Wilmot's proviso in 1846, Congress was deluged by

> petitions and resolutions of legislatures in the Northern states, and popular meetings, to exclude the Southern states from all territories acquired, or to be acquired, and to prevent the admission of any state hereafter into the Union, which by its Constitution does not prohibit slavery.

What, asked Calhoun, was the meaning of all this? The antislavery people, he charged, had made no secret of their views. All of this was just a beginning; the ultimate goal of the movement was not merely to check the growth of slavery in the territories but to abolish it entirely, wherever it existed. Calhoun again asked,

> what is to stop this agitation, unless something decisive is done, before the great and final objective at which it aims—the abolition of slavery in the South—is consummated? Is it not certain that if something decisive is not now done to arrest it, the South will be forced to choose between abolition and secession?

Yes, the nightmare which the slaveholders had been living with since the creation of the Union was now turning into reality. Northern opinion was beginning to challenge the slaveholder's hitherto unchallenged control both of his black chattels and of the federal government itself. Northern opinion, so long silent and passive on the issue of slavery, was beginning to stir. Antislavery opinion was on the way to becoming majority opinion. And how long would it be before these northern antislavery whites, to accomplish their purposes, joined forces with the black slaves themselves, still toiling anonymously, quietly, and reluctantly in the southern fields?

How, then, could the Union be saved? Calhoun's conclusion was somber, and his advice to the slaveholding South was grim. The Union cannot be saved. Secede now, get out, decide by war who is to rule and control the American Republic and its western lands.

The advice was revolutionary, but it was not new. Calhoun dwelt at length, and lovingly, on the example of a great and revolutionary slaveholder, George Washington. There was a Union while that great man was growing up, he said,

that between the parent country and her then colonies. It was a Union that had much to endear it to the people of the colonies. Under its protecting and superintending care, the colonies were planted and grew up and prospered through a long course of years, until they became populous and wealthy. . . . Washington was born and grew up to manhood under that Union. He acquired his early distinction in its service, and there is every reason to believe that he was devotedly attached to it. But his devotion was a rational one. He was attached to it, not as an end, but as a means to an end. When it failed to fulfil its end and, instead of affording protection, was converted into the means of oppressing the colonies, he did not hesitate to draw his sword, and head the great movement by which that Union was forever severed, and the independence of these states established. This was the great and crowning glory of his life. . . .

Follow Washington's example, Calhoun was telling the slaveholders. Declare your independence and enforce it with the sword. What will follow? Like the revolutionaries of 1776, you will inherit the American land. You have ruled the Union, and it has offered you, so far, many advantages. Now it challenges your power. Ruin it, and build another of your own.

To underline his point that secession was now necessary, inevitable, and right, Calhoun sketched the demands that the South should make as a condition of remaining within the Union, conditions, as he well knew, which the North could not fulfill:

—Do not admit California to the Union until she has written a constitution that permits the entrance of slavery.
—Stop the agitation against slavery.
—Pass a constitutional amendment giving the South the power to veto acts of Congress of which she does not approve.

Within a month, Calhoun was dead. Democrats, both northern and southern, recoiled from the path he pointed out, leading directly to the chasm. Under the leadership of Senator Stephen Douglas of Illinois, they redoubled their efforts to reach an agreement. In August and September 1850, following the death of President Taylor, five bills were passed through Congress embodying what has become known to history as the Compromise of 1850.

This compromise was a treaty of peace between the sections, and it followed in principle the proposals submitted to Congress by Henry Clay in January. California was admitted as a free state, counterbalancing the admission of Texas as a slave state. New Mexico was thrown open to slave settlement; slavery was abolished in the District of Columbia. Civil war and the destruction of the Union were, for the time being, avoided.

Perhaps the most important part of the Compromise of 1850 was a new Fugitive Slave Act which spelled out the way in which the full power and authority of the federal government was to be placed at the disposal of slaveholders seeking the capture and return of fugitive slaves.

We saw earlier that the free states, outraged by the *Prigg* decision that denied jury trial to people accused of being fugitives, were passing during the 1840s a new type of liberty law—laws that forbade state officials to co-operate in any way with the federal government in bringing about the return to the South of fugitives. Very well: the new Fugitive Slave Act enlarged the power of the federal government to catch slaves and spelled out how this power was to be exercised. Special federal commissioners were to be appointed by the federal courts with authority to hear cases involving fugitives and to issue certificates of release to the masters applying for them. Commissioners were to be paid a ten dollar fee for every fugitive they turned over to his owner; if they found that a black person alleged to be a fugitive was not, their fee was to be only five dollars. If an owner feared that his slave might be forcibly liberated on the way home by angry antislavery people, the federal government itself was authorized to take charge of the slave and deliver him safely back to the plantation. "And to this end," said the act, the federal official was

hereby authorized and required to employ so many persons as he may deem necessary to overcome such force, and to retain them in his service so long as circumstances may require. The said officer and his assistants, while so employed, to receive the same compensation, and to be allowed the same expenses, as are now allowed by law for transportation of criminals, to be certified by the judge of the district within which the arrest is made, and paid out of the treasury of the United States.

The act meant exactly what it said. The army, navy, and the marines were now at the disposal of the slave-holders for the return of their property. And the cost was to be borne by the American taxpayer. As we shall see later, in the case of Anthony Burns in 1854, it would take an entire regiment to return one single human being to the South.

Where called upon, federal marshals were authorized to make the arrest of fugitives and bring them before the commissioners; and they were empowered to enlist the help of anybody who happened to be around—"by-standers," the act called them—in making arrests. "All good citizens," said the act, "are hereby commanded to aid and assist in the prompt and efficient execution of the law, whenever their services may be required." The act openly and explicitly stated that black people accused of being fugitives from labor did not have the right to a jury trial in federal court or the right to testify on their own behalf—no Fifth Amendment rights for them. "In no trial or hearing under this act," said section 6, "shall the testimony of such alleged fugitive be admitted in evidence."

Southerners regarded this act as the acid test of northern good faith. Would the federal government carry out its commitment? Would the North permit it?

Boston poster of 1851, urging defiance of
the new fugitive slave law.

The Fugitive Slave Act was passed on September 18, 1850. Two months later, on November 18, Judge Kane of the Federal Circuit Court in Philadelphia told the grand jury that on account of this measure "the country has been convulsed in its length and breadth, as if about to be rent asunder, and tossed in fragments, by the outbursting of a volcano."

What the judge meant was made clear by events that occurred at Christiana, Lancaster County, on September 11, 1851, when a band of black men, some one hundred strong, killed a Maryland slaveholder, Edward Gorsuch, who sought to arrest his fugitive slaves, and chased away the people who were with him, including the federal marshal, Henry Kline.

September 11 was a morning when a heavy mist hung over Christiana in the lovely Chester Valley. Shortly after daybreak, Edward Gorsuch and Henry Kline, with five others, were seen approaching the house of William Parker, a black man. A great blowing of tin horns, and hallooing, warned the entire countryside of their approach.

Gorsuch's party arrived at the house and began to negotiate with the black people inside. Gorsuch called his slaves by name, said that he had warrants for their arrest, and promised that if they came quietly, "he would treat them kindly and forget the past." Some ten minutes were taken up in these negotiations; in the meantime, an angry crowd of black people—farm workers, blacksmiths' apprentices, and the like—had gathered.

Among those who arrived on the scene was Castner Hanway, the miller of Christiana; he had ridden over to find out what the fuss was about—was this a kidnaping of the kind that Pennsylvanians were all too familiar with, or was it a legal arrest in accordance with the Fugitive Slave Act of 1850? Kline walked up to Hanway and ordered him to assist in making the arrests. Hanway refused.

Dr. Pierce, a member of Gorsuch's party, was frightened by the threatening attitude of the crowd; he implored Gorsuch to leave. The party moved down the lane, leading away from the house.

Then, as Dr. Pierce described it,

In coming out of the short lane, when [Dr. Pierce] had persuaded the old gentleman to leave, [Dr. Pierce] found his [Gorsuch's] countenance had changed; he looked calm and stern, and he wheeled around and said he would have his slaves or he would die in the attempt. The old gentleman stepped three or four paces, advanced toward the negroes, and received a wound and fell.

Edward Gorsuch, fatally wounded, soon died. Dickinson Gorsuch, his son, was also hurt.

Thirty-eight people were arrested as a result of this death. Castner Hanway was the first to be taken into custody and, as it proved, the only person to be placed on trial by the federal government. On November 25, 1851, a little more than one year after the passage of the Fugitive Slave Act, he was arraigned in Constitution Hall, Philadelphia, and charged with the crime of high treason in that he did "wickedly and traitorously prevent, by means of force and intimidation, the execution of the Fugitive Slave Act." In that same building, sixty-four years before, Pierce Butler had proposed the fugitive

The struggle at Christiana, 1851.

slave clause and had had it written into the Constitution with little opposition.

Castner Hanway's trial was one of the longest and most important in the history of American criminal law. Among the lawyers who defended him was Thaddeus Stevens of Lancaster. Hanway's crime was not that he had counseled or organized resistance to the Fugitive Slave Law, but that he had refused to join the federal government in laying hands upon fugitive slaves and had refused to help the government in returning such people to bondage. On December 16, 1851, the jury delivered their verdict: *not guilty*.

Enforcement of the Fugitive Slave Act did not encounter in many places such furious resistance as at Christiana. But while Hanway's trial was going on, Harriet Stowe, writing in Brunswick, Maine, was completing *Uncle Tom's Cabin*. This book broadcast the lesson of Hanway's trial to thousands of northerners. Resistance to tyranny, wrote Mrs. Stowe, is obedience to God.

DO AS YOU WOULD BE DONE BY
Harriet Stowe and Uncle Tom's Cabin, 1853

Slavery is not lawful, for it does not conform to God's rule, do as you would be done by.

Samuel Sewall, *The Selling of Joseph*

The Fugitive Slave Act of 1850 was passed by Congress on September 18. Just four months earlier, Harriet Beecher Stowe, then thirty-nine years old, had arrived at Brunswick, Maine, after a long, exhausting trip overland from Cincinnati, and had taken up residence at the Titcomb House. That same month her seventh child, Charles Edward, was born. Early the following year, in February 1851, while the child still lay in his cradle, Mrs. Stowe set to work on a novel, *Uncle Tom's Cabin*. In June of that year the story began to appear in serial form in an antislavery newspaper, the *National Era*. In 1852 it was published as a two volume paperback by Jewett of Boston.

Uncle Tom's Cabin was a bold attack on slavery. Well over one million copies sold in the United States alone before the beginning of the Civil War, and the book was translated into thirty or more foreign languages. Southerners, understandably, were unhappy about this, and there were angry reviews in southern journals. But nobody threw rocks at Mrs. Stowe like they had at Theodore Weld. The *National Era* was printed in Washington, D.C.; nobody attacked its press as they had James Birney's, and threw it into the Potomac. Nobody said that a woman who dared to make an onslaught upon slavery even more sustained and passionate than Garrison's should be "put to death without benefit of clergy."

What were the reasons for Mrs. Stowe's great success? What part did her literary work play in the developing struggle between the slaveholders and the American people, and why?

Harriet Beecher, like so many other antislavery leaders, was a New Englander. Born at Litchfield, Connecticut, in 1811, she grew up with a deep love for New England, its sights, its sounds, its people. Among the most precious of her childhood memories was the lovely Connecticut Valley and its encircling hills. "I remember," she recalled, "standing in the door of our house and looking over a distant horizon where Mount Tom reared its round blue head against the sky, and the Great and Little Ponds, as they were called, gleamed out amid a steel-blue sea of distant pine groves."

Harriet's mother, Roxana Beecher, died when the little girl was only five. She remembered the consolation offered her by Candace, the black washwoman. "She drew me towards her," wrote Harriet, "and held me quite still . . . and then she kissed my hand, and I felt her tears drop on it."

So the child grew up in a house full of boys—her older brothers, William, Edward, and George; and the younger ones, Henry Ward and Charles. They were the playmates of her youth and her lifelong friends. The days when Reverend Lyman Beecher, their father, took the boys off on all-male fishing trips were dark ones for Harriet. She stayed by herself in the quiet house. "All day," she recalled,

it was so still; no tramping or laughing, wrestling boys— no singing and shouting; and perhaps only a long seam on a sheet to be oversewed as the sole means of beguiling the hours of absence. . . . And then what joy to hear at a distance the tramp of feet, the shouts and laughs of older brothers; and what glad triumph when the successful party burst into the kitchen with long strings of perch, roach, pickerel, and bullheads, with waving blades of sweet-flag, and high heads of cattail, and pockets full of young wintergreen. . . .

Harriet lived in her father's home in Litchfield until she was fourteen. Then she went to Hartford as a pupil in the Female Academy on Main Street, which was run by her older sister, Catharine, and which had already won fame as one of the most distinguished experimental schools for young women in the country. In a little while, before she was seventeen, Harriet was herself a teacher in that school.

In the meantime, events were being set in motion that would have an important influence on the life of the whole Beecher family. By 1830 all the Christian denominations were sending ministers to the West, and endowing western colleges to train young men to give spiritual

Harriet Beecher Stowe during
her Cincinatti residence.

leadership in the great new land beyond the Appalachians. The Presbyterians, as we saw earlier, founded Lane Seminary in Cincinnati for this purpose in 1829; there was general agreement among them that Harriet's father, Reverend Lyman Beecher, would be the most suitable man to head this new college. Lyman Beecher was a famous Puritan minister. As one of Lane's founders put it, he was "the most prominent, popular, and powerful preacher in the nation"; the magnetism of his presence and leadership, it was hoped, would "draw together young men from every part of our country."

Lyman Beecher accepted the call to Lane Seminary in 1832, two years after his son Edward had become president of Illinois College at Jacksonville. Almost the whole family moved west with him. There was Lyman himself, his sister Esther, and his second wife, Harriet Porter, with her three children, Isabella, Thomas, and James. There was Harriet's older brother George, who was to take up a post as minister at Chillicothe, Ohio. As for Harriet and Catharine, they planned to work together and to establish a new girls' school—Western Female Seminary, as it was called—in Cincinnati.

And so the Beecher family came to Lane Seminary in November 1832 and took up residence at the college located at Walnut Hills, a couple of miles outside Cincinnati. Harriet lived there for a little more than seventeen years, first in her father's house and, after her marriage in 1836, in her own home close by. Harriet taught school for a while and then married Lane's Bible professor, Calvin Ellis Stowe, to whom she bore seven children. Calvin Stowe was a native of Massachusetts, and nine years older than his wife. He was a graduate of

Andover Theological Seminary, and a very scholarly individual—he knew Latin, Greek, German, and Hebrew. Many months of his life, while the Stowes were living in Cincinnati, were spent in travel. In 1836 the state of Ohio sent him to Europe to make a study of the German educational system; later he traveled as an agent of Lane College in, for the most part, a fruitless search for new funds. Calvin Stowe was a mild, absent-minded man who was most at home among his books. Taken up with his travels and his study and his teaching, he offered Harriet little support in the daily trials of her existence. It was a dull, narrow existence made wretched by poverty, ill health, and household drudgery. Harriet herself summed it up later. "During these long years," she wrote, "of struggling with poverty and sickness and a hot debilitating climate my children grew up around me. The nursery and the kitchen were my principal fields of labor."

Of course, this domestic existence was only one aspect of Harriet's life. Like many talented women in a similar situation, she was in constant revolt against a life of apron strings. Like other women of intelligence and sensitivity, she was keenly aware of events in the wider world around her; she had time, amid the endless daily routine, to ponder their meaning.

The continuing reality of Harriet's Cincinnati experience was the crisis and the struggle over slavery. The Lane Antislavery Society, as we saw earlier, was suppressed in the summer of 1834, scarcely two years after the arrival of the Beecher family. James G. Birney arrived in Cincinnati in 1835 and proceeded to publish a new antislavery organ, the *Philanthropist*. In July 1836, an

The wrecking of an abolitionist press,
from a contemporary woodcut.

orgy of mob violence broke out. Birney's office was smashed and his press thrown into the river; innocent black people were then assaulted in the Cincinnati ghetto. Furniture and broken glass littered the streets, doors were ripped off, whole houses demolished. As Harriet described it to Calvin, who was away at the time,

the mob tore down Birney's press, scattered his types, and then came back to demolish the office. . . . The "lads" spent the rest of the night and a greater part of the next day, Sunday, in pulling down the houses of inoffensive and respectable blacks.

Soon the crisis was over, but for Harriet the experience was instructive. It underlined something that the academic-freedom struggle at Lanc in 1834 had begun to make clear. Slavery in America was more than just the physical fact that there were chains upon the legs and arms of black people; slavery was an *all-American* institution whose law and power were a force far beyond the borders of the South.

Hard upon the heels of the 1836 riots came another, and for Harriet even more important, antislavery experience. In August 1836, before Birney's press had hardly had time to settle on the river bottom, Elijah Lovejoy arrived in Cincinnati to make arrangements to replace the press that had just been destroyed by Missourians at Alton. Lovejoy, as we remember, lost his life scarcely a year later—on November 7, 1837, while defending his press, and his freedom to use it, by force of arms.

This clash at Alton between the Puritan minister and the power of slavery was an episode of high significance in the life of the American people. But for Harriet

Stowe the story of Elijah Lovejoy had a very special meaning. Edward Beecher, who played a leading role in the drama at Alton, was Harriet's older brother, and the two had been especially close since childhood. She adored Edward, and looked up to him with love and deep respect for his human sympathy and his sturdy common sense. "Somehow or other," Harriet wrote to Edward when she was still a teen-ager, "you have such a reasonable sort of way of saying things that when I come to reflect I almost always go over to your side."

Lyman Beecher, Harriet and Edward's father, had turned his back on the antislavery movement at Lane. Lyman saw Weld and his debates as an embarrassing and controversial obstacle in his efforts to build a solid and respectable midwestern school. But, through Edward, Harriet became linked to the very movement that her father rejected, and she became deeply involved in it. Elijah Lovejoy died at Alton just a few hours after Edward Beecher had left him. This was for Harriet a terrifying and revealing experience. She read, and read again, Edward's little pamphlet, *Narrative of Riots at Alton*. She marked his conclusions, and she made them her own. The antislavery cause, Edward had said, was a manifestation of God's will. Lovejoy's martyrdom was like a cloud-shadow moving across the New England hills; it was God's mark upon the land, His warning to the American people, His motion in history.

The more clearly Harriet began to understand the meaning of the struggle against slavery that was developing in the United States during the 1830s and '40s, the more intolerable did her own personal position become. Through both her father and her husband she was bound up with an institution, Lane Seminary, that had forbidden discussion of the antislavery cause. Harriet ate the seminary's bread and was, therefore, part of the seminary's guilt. She addressed, in 1837, an agonized question to Calvin. "Pray," she asked him, "what is there in Cincinnati to satisfy one whose mind is awakened on this subject? No one can have the system of slavery brought before him without an irrepressible desire to *do* something, and what is there to be done?"

The answer for her at that time, of course, was: Nothing! Her twins, Harriet and Eliza, had been born in 1836, a little more than a year before Lovejoy was assassinated. Henry Ellis arrived in January 1838, followed by Frederick William in May 1840, Georgiana May in August 1843, and Samuel Charles in January 1848. The harassed mother wrote to Calvin in 1844 an account of her typical morning routine:

Rise at half-past five—breakfast at six. Morning prayer til seven. Work in garden til eight—then come in the house, review knives, spoons, castors and all the table paraphernalia—count and see that everything is in proper order—half-past nine, call the children in to school, sing a hymn, pray with them, and give them a bible lesson half an hour long. . . . Then read in a class and sew til dinner time.

Through such a routine a woman might fulfill her duty to her family, but it did violence to her new-found convictions and ideals as a human being. She thought, what about a woman's duty to God? And duty to God, what was it, but to throw yourself into the struggle against human bondage?

Flight was a possibility that the Stowes discussed with each other, but they ruled it out for a number of reasons. Principally, it did not seem right to abandon Lane when the college was heavily in debt, leaving Lyman, who in 1840 was sixty-five, to struggle alone with the burden. "It was thought," said Harriet,

that we must not leave the position, but struggle on with what hope we might, til the institution should be clear from debt. It was the hardest trial of our life, at this time, to be obliged to refuse continued invitations to return to New England.

So Harriet and Calvin hung grimly on, wavering between the wild desire to leave and the sense of loyalty that bade them stay. And always, during the 1830s and '40s, when the Stowes were trapped in Cincinnati, the evil of slavery in the nation grew worse. Harriet reared her growing family against an ominous backdrop of mounting tension and crisis. In 1845 Texas was annexed by joint resolution of Congress and thrown open to slavery. The war against Mexico followed, ending with a sweeping U.S. victory; the defeated country was compelled to surrender at sword's point a vast territory lying between the Rio Grande and the Pacific. In 1849 Congress began to debate the future of this vast domain, and slaveholders began to talk openly of war and secession if their rights in the new lands were not honored. Harriet's sense of her own impotence, her feeling of guilt in the face of encroaching evil, was heightened by these events.

Harriet's predicament during these years led to deep inner conflict which expressed itself in chronic ill health and nervous prostration. She complained of splitting

The Cincinatti waterfront, 1838.

headaches, of unbearable pain in the eyes when the light was bright. The symptoms all vanished when she went for a year's rest to Brattleboro, Vermont, in 1846. Walking alone amid the frozen beauty of the New England winter, she looked back to the days of her virgin dreams and uttered a cry of anguish for the shattered hopes of the intervening years. "No creature," she mourned, "ever so longed to see the face of a little one or had such a heart full of love to bestow. . . . *Ah, how little comfort had I in being a mother!*"

Not long after Harriet's return from Vermont, a terrible epidemic of cholera swept Cincinnati. Cincinnati, like other western cities, paid a high price in human life for its rapid, unregulated growth. The houses of the well-to-do were brick, but the wooden tenements of the poor were crammed close together, and this increased the risk of disastrous fires. Vile sanitary and drainage facilities posed a menace to health. Swamps and marshes along the riverfront were breeding grounds for mosquitoes; sewage accumulating in stagnant pools generated pestilential diseases. The annual death-rate from fever was high; at times it reached epidemic proportions. At frequent intervals the people suffered the horrors of the plague. Its ghastly manifestations—endless funeral processions, blazing coals at the crossroads, uncoffined corpses in wheelbarrows and country carts—were a part of nineteenth-century Cincinnati experience.

In the summer of 1849 cholera was claiming more than one thousand victims every week. The corpses were borne, in an unending stream, to the graveyard. Harriet watched the grisly scene from her window. "The air," she wrote to Calvin, who in his turn was enjoying a

Vermont rest cure, "was of that peculiarly oppressive deathly kind that seems to lie like lead on the brain and soul."

By the beginning of July there was rising panic in the city. The mayor, on the advice of the clergy, declared July 3 a "day of general fasting, humiliation and prayer." Many people, in those days, thought of epidemic disease as a punishment sent by God for sin, as a warning that sinners should repent and change their ways. On such a fast day as July 3 you prayed for mercy, and you told God that you were truly sorry for your sins.

One week after the day of fasting, humiliation, and prayer, Harriet's youngest child, Samuel Charles, then eighteen months old, was taken ill. Before the end of the month she wrote to Calvin to tell him that his son was at the point of death. "I have just seen him," she wrote,

in his death agony, looking on his imploring face when I could not help or soothe nor do one thing, not one, to mitigate his cruel suffering, do nothing but pray in my anguish that he might die soon. I write as though there were no sorrow like my sorrow, yet there has been in this city, as in the land of Egypt, scarce a house without its dead.

The comparison of cholera in Cincinnati to the plague in Egypt was a flash in which Mrs. Stowe, speaking at a moment of agony, lit up her inmost soul. The sin for which the Egyptians were punished was the refusal of their Pharaoh to release the Jewish slaves. God's warning against slavery was to be seen in Cincinnati in a universal death that found, for Harriet, its focus in the tiny shrouded corpse that lay in her own home.

In August the plague diminished in intensity. In September Calvin came back from New England with the news that he had been offered a professorship at Bowdoin College in Brunswick, Maine. Now, after the long years of waiting, the Stowes could return home from exile. Lyman Beecher would follow soon after, for now he was an old man and the time for his retirement had come; in 1851 he took up his residence at Hayward Place in Boston. Yes, the years of exile were finally over. Harriet, at last, was free to write and to act against slavery.

Thus it was that Harriet Stowe left Cincinnati in April 1850 for the long trip east, taking with her Henry and Hattie, and leaving the rest of the family to follow in June. She reached Brunswick in May and was warmly greeted by the Bowdoin faculty, who had engaged the Titcomb House for her and her family. "The house," she wrote to Calvin, "is in a very good state of repair, and considering that it is a *chance hit* suits our purposes wonderfully." True, the rent was more than she had expected to pay, but this did not worry Harriet unduly. "As I mean," she told her husband "to raise a sum myself equivalent to the rent this year, it only imposes the labor of writing an extra piece or two."

In this house the family was reunited, June 1850. Here, that same month, Charles Edward was born, almost exactly one year after the death of Samuel Charles in Cincinnati. Three months later, on September 18, 1850, the second Fugitive Slave Act became law. Early in 1851, just as Mrs. Stowe was beginning composition of the *Cabin*, Boston began to be rocked by mass resistance to the new law, and by the struggle to free two fugitives from federal custody: Fred Jenkins, who was rescued and sent on to Canada in February, and Thomas Sims who was arrested by the federal officials and returned to his Georgia master in April.

Thus, 1850 was a crucial year in the development of the sectional conflict and in the advance of the mass movement against slavery. Precisely at this time, Harriet was liberated from Lane. The dam was broken; the passionate indignation and the pent-up dreams of sixteen years came roaring through the breach.

Composition of the *Cabin* began early in 1851. The bulky novel was finished in a year. All the necessary conditions for the creation of the book were present: an audience awakened to the dangers of an expansionist slave power, and ready to be unified in opposition to it; literary talent that rose to brilliance in the creation of realistic dialogue; a wealth of information about the impact of slavery on the American people, drawn from seventeen years' residence on the borders of the slave empire; and, finally, an author suddenly released from restraint and eager, for the complex reasons we have begun to probe, to play more than an observer's role in the developing conflict.

Uncle Tom's Cabin enjoyed an amazing popularity in the decade before the outbreak of the Civil War. What, we need to ask ourselves, was the secret of its phenomenal success?

Was the book an indictment of the physical brutality of slavery? Hardly; there is violence in the *Cabin*, to be sure, but it is not a catalogue of horrors. Two out of three of Mrs. Stowe's leading slaveholders, Shelby and

St. Clare, are shown as kind and considerate men. Only Legree is painted as a brute.

Was the *Cabin* an attempt to show the actual life of slaves, or, as Theodore Weld put it, "their food, clothing, lodging, dwellings, hours of labor and rest . . . treatment when sick, regulations respecting their social intercourse, marriage and domestic ties"? There is almost nothing of this sort in the book. Equally clear is a lack of interest, on the author's part, in exploring the psychological realities of oppression endured by black people— the experience of fear, sorrow, and rage that was the daily torment of a slave.

Was it Mrs. Stowe's purpose to show the sufferings of fugitives? The image of the *Cabin* that remains in the minds of many people is that of Eliza crossing the ice, baby in arms and bloodhounds baying behind. This seems to make sense. Is not the novel, after all, a tract against the Fugitive Slave Act and the crime of hunting human beings? Does not the book symbolize, in the person of the fugitive, the political menace of a slave power that has seized control of the federal law itself?

Take up the *Cabin*, read it, and mark the space that Mrs. Stowe gives to the fugitive theme. Only about 70 of its 450 pages are given up to tell the story of Eliza and her George. As for the famous incident of Eliza crossing the Ohio by leaping, babe in arms, from floe to floe, Harriet gets the young woman across the river in two quick paragraphs. Not in her wildest dreams would the author have guessed that this incident would make the fortunes of traveling Tom shows for half a century. So our confusion deepens; the fugitive theme is a minor one, after all.

Perhaps the most useful clue to the task that Mrs. Stowe set for herself in the *Cabin* was a remark she made in a letter she wrote in 1853 to a North Carolina abolitionist, Daniel Goodloe. "I have endeavored," she wrote, "to separate the system from the men."

By 1850 the American people throughout the North, not just abolitionists, were discovering that slavery, as a system of organized rule, was becoming dangerous to them; they were becoming, far more than they had been during the 1830s or '40s, receptive to the idea that this system was not only a political menace but also fundamentally immoral. This conclusion, that slavery was both dangerous and evil, found its way, in the few years that followed publication of the *Cabin,* into the minds and hearts of millions of Americans. It was a *moral* conclusion which in the course of time would have *military* consequences. It was here, then, that Mrs. Stowe made her contribution: she made a moral judgment upon a system; she held this system up against the framework of traditional Christian morality and ethics, and she judged it accordingly.

A Christian judgment upon slavery and all its works, of course, was in itself nothing new—since the eighteenth century abolitionist agitators, and in particular Quakers and New Englanders, had been attacking slavery as something contrary to the laws both of God and man. But the form of Mrs. Stowe's attack differed from that of previous moralists. She painted a series of scenes, and there set the system in motion. She introduced living, breathing people onto her stage, and showed how the *system,* even when individual slaveholders were kind, decent people, ground its victims up, body and soul, and destroyed them. At each point she took the law sanctioning property in man and set it against the law and command of God with respect to the *human* use of human beings. She showed how the system of slavery abused humanity, how it trampled upon the Puritan Christian ethic that was the bedrock of the American community. And this she did in a series of tracts in scenic procession, in a nineteenth-century morality play.

What kind of abolitionist was Mrs. Stowe? We might call her a conservative abolitionist. She differed from the radicals like Garrison because she offered no clear picture at all of the steps that the American people ought to take in order to rid themselves of the evil of the slavery system. As for the future of black people once slavery was abolished she had only the haziest of ideas; she shared, in fact, the views of the colonizationists who thought that they should all be shipped back to Africa. In all this, as we shall see, her position was extremely close to that of Abraham Lincoln and simply expressed the current feelings of millions of ordinary Americans.

No, the thrust of the *Cabin* did not lie in its radical vision of an American interracial future; it lay elsewhere. It was a call to Americans to place themselves in harmony with their *own* religion, their *own* Declaration of Independence, to recognize simply that the holding of men and women in bondage, regardless of race, creed, or color, was *wrong* and must stop. She blew a blast upon an evangelical clarion announcing the end of a world— the world of slavery. In doing this she saw herself as a messenger of God bearing tidings both of doom and joy. She announced, and she demanded, a revolution in American public opinion.

It was precisely the same kind of revolution in American opinion that Tom Paine had engineered when he wrote *Common Sense,* pointing out the inevitability and the necessity for the American colonies to separate from England. It was this revolution in public opinion that John Calhoun had foreseen, that had given him nightmares, and that he understood would mark the beginning of the end of slavery as a dominant American institution. Because he understood, in 1850, that this great change in opinion was about to be accomplished, he had called with his dying breath for secession and war.

American opinion was ripe for this revolution. It was due largely to Mrs. Stowe that it occurred exactly when it did. The sectional collision loomed. She translated it into human and moral terms that millions of ordinary people could measure, feel, and understand.

OUTER DARKNESS
Dred Scott v. Sanford, 1857

Cast ye the unprofitable servant into outer darkness: there shall be weeping and gnashing of teeth.

Saint Matthew

On May 24, 1854, Anthony Burns was seized on Brattle Street, Boston, within a stone's throw of Faneuil Hall, and thrust into jail. The warrant for his arrest as a fugitive slave had been signed by Edward G. Loring, an official of the government of the United States. On June 2, just nine days later, an armed escort of a thousand men surrounded Burns as he was marched down to the dock and placed on board a steamer bound for Virginia. The First Battalion of Light Dragoons, the Fifth Regiment of Artillery, the Fifth Regiment of Light Infantry, the Third Battalion of Light Infantry, and the Corps of Cadets were pressed into service by the federal government to hold back the people of Boston and to enforce the Fugitive Slave Act of 1850 against Anthony Burns. An observer described the scene before Burns was brought out and the parade began:

At eleven o'clock, Court Square presented a spectacle that became indelibly engraved upon the memories of men. The people had been swept out of the Square, and stood crowded together in Court Street, presenting to the eye a solid rampart of human beings. At the eastern door of the Court House, stood the cannon, loaded, and with its mouth pointed full upon the compact mass. . . . It was the first time that the armed power of the United States had ever been arrayed against the people of Massachusetts.

All this it took, in June 1854, to manacle a single runaway and ship him south.

This bold defiance of slaveholders' law, was it something special in 1854, something that happened only in Boston? Not at all. On May 30, at the very time when Burns' hearing was taking place in the Boston Court House, Congress passed the Kansas-Nebraska bill repealing the Missouri Compromise of 1820. This triggered a movement of protest against slavery that swept through every town and village of the North. The quiet that had settled over the land following the Compromise of 1850 was shattered.

The Missouri Compromise had provided for the future of the territory purchased from France in 1803; it settled the question of slavery in the Louisiana Purchase.

The Louisiana Purchase, accomplished in Thomas Jefferson's first administration, doubled the size of the United States. Purchase lands stretched from the waters of the Mississippi a thousand miles westward to the foothills of the Rockies, from the Canadian borderlands a thousand miles southward to the plains of Texas. Except for the area around the port of New Orleans, the

The federal army and Anthony Burns, Boston, 1854.

Purchase lands were unexplored by white men, the home of the wandering Indian people and the buffalo. But the precise boundaries of the Purchase were settled by diplomatic negotiations with Spain and Great Britain in 1818–1819.

In 1819 Missouri settlers applied for admission to the Union as a state, and submitted for the approval of Congress a constitution legalizing slavery. This produced a crisis. The admission of Missouri with slavery would set a precedent for the future settlement of the entire area. If slavery were made legal in Missouri, people asked, why could it not penetrate everywhere else in the Purchase?

After a lot of squabbling and discussion, Congress reached a compromise. Missouri was admitted as a slave state, balanced by Maine as a free state. The rest of the Louisiana Purchase territory was split into two zones, or "spheres of interest," one zone for the slaveholders and one for free settlers. The dividing line was set at 36° 30′ north latitude. In all lands below that parallel of latitude, and within Louisiana Purchase territory, slavery was declared legal. In all lands above that parallel, with the exception, of course, of Missouri, slavery was banned.

Some southerners challenged the right of Congress to pass laws banning slavery in American territories. But Congress felt that its power to control the territories and their government was based upon the Constitution. Article IV, section 3, seemed to confer sovereignty, or exclusive authority over territories, upon Congress. "The Congress," said section 3, "shall have power to dispose of and make all needful rules and regulations respecting the territory or other property belonging to the United States."

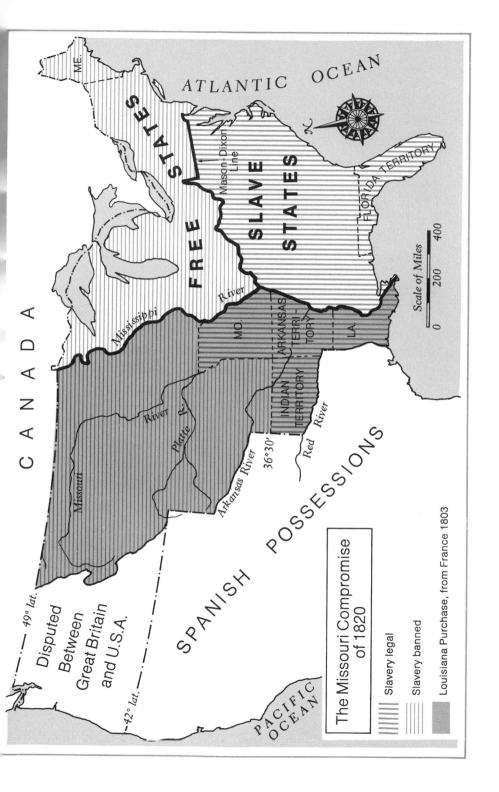

The Missouri Compromise of 1820

Slavery legal

Slavery banned

Louisiana Purchase, from France 1803

In the course of time nine free states would be carved out of the free territory above 36°30′: Montana, Iowa, Minnesota, North Dakota, South Dakota, Kansas, Nebraska, Wyoming, and Colorado. One slave state, Arkansas, would be formed from slave territory south of 36°30′. For the moment everybody was satisfied, more or less. The South had won a *precedent*, that new lands west of the Mississippi might be admitted to the Union with slavery. Congress had succeeded in affirming its control over the Purchase lands, and in banning slavery from most of them.

The Kansas-Nebraska Act of 1854 upset this Compromise of 1820 that had lasted thirty-five years, and swept it away. North of 36°30′ in the Purchase the act created two territories, Kansas Territory and Nebraska Territory. People who settled in these lands, even though they were *all* north of 36°30′, were given the option of choosing whether or not they wanted slavery. In effect the act said: "the federal government doesn't care whether there is slavery or not in these territories. The matter will be decided by the first settlers who get there, who organize a territorial government, and who vote for or against the existence of slavery in their community. What can be more democratic than that?"

The Kansas-Nebraska bill had been introduced and driven through Congress by Stephen Douglas, U.S. senator from Illinois, the top Democratic party chieftain now that Calhoun was dead. The bill was the result of a deal between the northern and southern wings of the Democratic party. Northern Democrats got a transcontinental railroad to California along a central route projected to run through Kansas. The southern Demo-

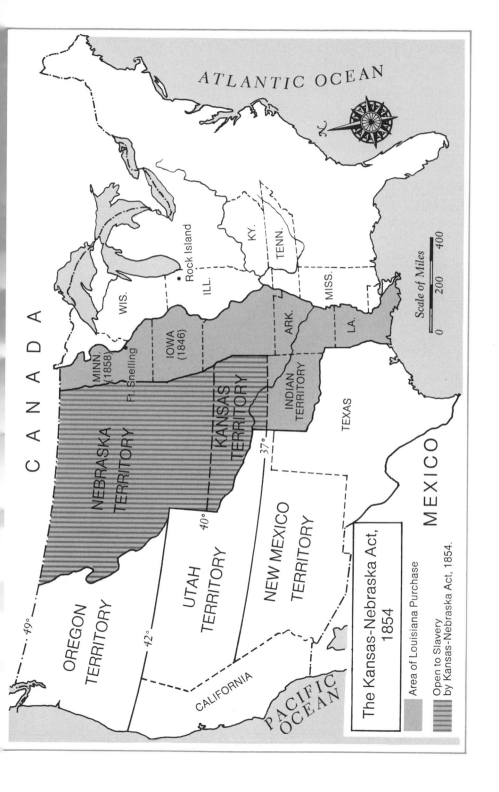

ATLANTIC OCEAN

CANADA

WIS.
• Rock Island
ILL.
KY.
TENN.
MINN. (1858)
Ft. Snelling
IOWA (1846)
ARK.
MISS.
LA.
KANSAS TERRITORY
INDIAN TERRITORY
NEBRASKA TERRITORY
TEXAS
37°
40°
OREGON TERRITORY
UTAH TERRITORY
NEW MEXICO TERRITORY
42°
49°
CALIFORNIA
MEXICO

PACIFIC OCEAN

Scale of Miles
0   200   400

The Kansas-Nebraska Act, 1854

Area of Louisiana Purchase

Open to Slavery
by Kansas-Nebraska Act, 1854.

crats abandoned their demand for a southern route in return for the rubbing out of the 36°30′ barrier and the opening up of Louisiana Purchase lands to slavery.

The result was predictable. In California the slave-holders had been beaten to the punch by the droves of free settlers who flocked to the state in search of gold and set up a state government banning slavery. This time, the southerners were determined to get their licks in first. People streamed across the border from Missouri; proslavery settlers announced to the world that Kansas was theirs:

We will afford protection to no abolitionist as a settler of this territory; we recognize the institution of slavery as already existing in this territory, and advise slave-holders to introduce their property as soon as possible.

The slavery people held elections for a territorial legislature in March 1855, importing thousands of "settlers" who made the round trip from Missouri just to vote. Hundreds of armed men camped around the anti-slavery center of Lawrence, beat up or chased away antislavery voters. The result was a victory for slavery. There were 1,400 settlers in Kansas qualified to vote, but 6,000 votes were cast, most of them by the visitors from Missouri. The legislature thus illegally elected, met and passed laws to legalize slavery and to put down those who opposed it by word or deed. Helping a slave escape from Kansas was to be punished by death.

The antislavery settlers fought back, set up their own legislature, and drafted an antislavery constitution. Thus, by the beginning of 1856, there were two governments in Kansas. In April 1856 civil war broke out when armed men from the southern states invaded the territory and sacked the town of Lawrence. White men were now fighting and killing white men over the issue of black slavery.

Almost two years to the day after the passage of the Kansas-Nebraska Act, Charles Sumner of Massachusetts rose in the United States Senate to denounce "the crime against Kansas" which he said, had been committed by Stephen Douglas and the Democrats. "It is," he said,

the rape of a virgin Territory, compelling it to the hateful embrace of slavery; and it may clearly be traced to a depraved longing for a new slave state, the hideous offspring of such a crime, in the hope of adding to the power of slavery in the national government. . . . Here in our republic, force—ay, sir, FORCE—has been openly employed in compelling Kansas to this pollution, and all for the sake of political power. . . . The creature, whose paws are now fastened upon Kansas constitutes in reality a part of the slavepower, which, in its loathsome folds, is now coiled about the whole land. . . . But out of the vastness of the crime attempted, with all its woe and shame, I derive a well-founded assurance of a commensurate vastness of effort against it by the aroused masses of the country.

Three days later Preston Brooks, congressman from South Carolina, attacked Sumner while sitting at his desk in the Senate, and beat him senseless. White men were now coming to blows about slavery not only on the plains of Kansas but in the halls of Congress itself.

Did Congress have the power, under Article IV, section 3, to ban slavery in the territories? Which side was right in Kansas—those fighting for slavery, or those against it?

Americans have long been accustomed to look to the Supreme Court for the settlement of both political and legal disputes. The slavery question was no exception. We saw earlier how in the *Prigg* case both sides looked to the Court for settlement of the dispute about the extradition of fugitives. In 1854 another case, *Dred Scott v. Sanford*, was working its way through the federal courts. The decision was handed down in 1857. It would provide an authoritative answer to the question that millions were asking.

The conflict of North and South, now grown to mighty proportions in Kansas, had its day in court. It was fought out around the person of a black slave, Dred Scott, and Dred Scott's wife, Harriet, and their two teen-age daughters, Lizzie and Eliza. These anonymous human beings now come forward to stand quietly in the very center of the American stage. They stand there very quietly as representatives of the black people, millions of them, around whom the struggle between slave and free was coming to its bloody, convulsive crisis.

How did the case of Dred, Harriet, Eliza, and Lizzie Scott arise; and why did it become so important?

There was a slave called Sam, who was born in Southampton County, Virginia. Sam's master, Peter Blow, emigrated from Southampton County in 1826, bringing Sam and a handful of other slaves to Saint Louis, Missouri. Peter Blow died in 1831, the year of Nat Turner's revolt, and Sam was sold to a Saint Louis resident, Dr. John Emerson, for $500. Two years later, Dr.

Emerson received an army commission and was assigned to Fort Armstrong on Rock Island in the state of Illinois. There he lived from 1834 to 1836 with his wife, Irene Emerson, and Sam.

In 1836 the army transferred Dr. Emerson to Fort Snelling, a military outpost far to the north in the Louisiana Purchase territory, and just above Pig's Eye, the trading post which would become one day the capital of the state of Minnesota. The fort was a grim, prison-like place built of stone, located on a high bluff on the western side of the Mississippi. The purpose of the place, and the regiment of federal troops who lived there, was to protect white settlers from the Sioux and Chippewa Indians whose hunting grounds they were invading and destroying.

Sam accordingly went with his master to this remote spot in federal territory where slavery was banned by the federal law. There he lived from 1836 to 1838. During this time he met Harriet, slave of Major Lawrence Talliaferro, the Indian agent at the fort. Harriet was sold by the major to Dr. Emerson, so that Harriet and Sam lived together as man and wife at the fort for two years. Eliza was born on the waters of the Mississippi, north of Missouri; Lizzie, in the state of Missouri.

In 1838 Dr. Emerson brought Sam and Harriet back to Missouri. Five years later the doctor died and his wife, Irene, inherited the small slave family. By the time of her husband's death Mrs. Emerson, like her contemporary Harriet Beecher Stowe, had been touched by the antislavery struggles of Saint Louis and the Ohio Valley; she had formed antislavery convictions. In 1846 she met and married Joseph Chaffee, a well-known

Massachusetts abolitionist, and went to live in New England. Her slaves, Sam Blow and his family, remained in Saint Louis.

Following Dr. Emerson's death in 1843, a small group of antislavery people in Saint Louis set up a test case around the person of Sam Blow and his family. At this point Sam changed his name, and he is known to history as Dred Scott. He probably did this in deference to Charlotte Blow, the daughter of Scott's original owner, Peter Blow, and now a leading member of the Saint Louis antislavery group. The publicity given to the case of a slave with her name would have constantly reminded Charlotte of her proslavery background.

The timing of this move is of great interest. The year of Dr. Emerson's death, 1843, was the year following the decision of the Supreme Court in *Prigg* v. *Pennsylvania*. By 1843, as we have seen, the question of the fugitive slave law had become central to the thinking and actions of the antislavery movement. *Prigg* denied those elementary safeguards of the Bill of Rights, the Fourth, Fifth, and Sixth Amendments, to black people accused of being fugitives. This denial of rights, following *Prigg*, was to be sustained and enforced by the authority of the federal government itself.

Prigg, as we have also seen, led to new conflicts between North and South. Antislavery lawyers, at the same time, were asking *other* questions about the rights of slaves; questions that, if presented to the courts, might trigger fresh legal and popular struggles on behalf of the rights of black men and women. What, they asked, is the position of a slave who does not *flee* to free soil but who is *taken there* by his owner, or *sent there* with his owner's permission and consent? Should not such a slave become free the moment he touches free soil? Freedom, these lawyers reasoned, is the law of the land. A slave entering a free state or a free territory where slavery is banned by law ought to become a free person as soon as he or she touches free soil, looks at a free sky, or breathes free air. Freedom, they said, is man's most celestial possession, but it is also a little bit like death. Once it happens to you, it is *an irreversible fact*; it can't be changed, it can't be undone or taken away.

Most slaveholders did not agree at all with this view of the matter. In the course of their daily lives they went back and forth across the border separating the free and slave states. Naturally they took their slaves with them to perform personal services and to nurse children; they sent slaves across the border as their agents to transact business. Slaveholders claimed and were granted "temporary residence privileges" for their slaves. The idea that this arrangement ought to be ended southerners found humiliating and unreasonable. Mr. Justice Scott, of the Supreme Court of Missouri, speaking in 1852, put it this way: Are we prepared, he asked, to allow the "law of freedom" to be enforced in southern courts?

On almost three sides the State of Missouri is surrounded by free soil. If one of our slaves touch that soil with his master's consent, he becomes entitled to his freedom. Considering the numberless incidents in which those living along an extreme frontier would have occasion to occupy their slaves beyond our boundary, how hard would it be if our courts should liberate all the slaves who should thus be employed. How unreasonable to ask it! If a master sends his slave to hunt his horses or

Dred Scott.

cattle beyond the boundary, shall he thereby be liberated?

What, then, ought to be the position of a slave taken or sent across the border with the consent of his owner? Did he become free? If he returned to a slave state, did he *retain* his right to freedom? Or could the law of slavery with equal right reclaim him and "reverse" his status? Such questions were not idle ones; the fate of thousands of slaves was affected by the answers the courts might give to them. So it is hardly surprising that the antislavery movement pressed such questions and sought court tests to provide answers.

The issues, naturally, were fought out state by state. Dred Scott's was just one of a number of such cases that came up before Pennsylvania, New York, Ohio, Illinois, Kentucky, and Missouri courts after 1840.

And so *Dred Scott* v. *Emerson* began its journey through the courts. Scott sued his owner for his freedom and for that of his family. His claim, as stated in the suit, was based upon the fact that Dr. Emerson "held him in servitude in the State of Illinois, and also in that territory ceded by France to the United States, under the name of Louisiana, which lies north of 36°30', north latitude, not included within the limits of the State of Missouri." There were two trials in state court, one in 1846 and one in 1850; in the second of these, the jury found for Scott. The case went on appeal to the Supreme Court of Missouri in 1852; the decision of the court below was reversed.

The State Supreme Court decision was a disappointment to Scott's antislavery backers. As of 1852, he was still legally a slave, and all his family were slaves—living in a free state and a free territory for four whole years had not made a bit of difference. There was no point, when this decision was handed down, in having other black Missouri slaves sue for freedom because they had been taken or sent to the free states.

Scott's antislavery backers decided to go for broke—to appeal the state decision as far as they could, all the way to the Supreme Court of the United States if possible. Since Irene Emerson's marriage to Joseph Chaffee, Scott and his family had been transferred to the ownership of Mrs. Emerson's brother, John Sanford, who was a resident of New York State. Scott, as a citizen of Missouri, now sued Sanford as a citizen of New York. By Article III, section 2, of the Constitution, suits between citizens of different states fall within the jurisdiction of the federal courts. What Scott said in his suit, in effect, was this: John Sanford, a citizen of New York, is holding me, Dred Scott, a citizen of Missouri, together with my wife, Harriet, and my children, Eliza and Lizzie, in captivity. I sue for release and for damages for this wrongful detention.

The case of *Dred Scott* v. *Sanford* reached the U.S. Circuit Court for the Missouri District in 1854, and was decided there on May 15—just two weeks before the passage of the Kansas-Nebraska Act nullifying the Missouri Compromise and the abolition of slavery in Louisiana Purchase territory. The jury found for Sanford; the case went on up to the U.S. Supreme Court.

It was 1856. The country was rocked by the question of Kansas; northerners were flocking there, rifles in hand, to defend the territory from the advance of the slave power. Now the slaveholders began to look to the Supreme Court to quiet the agitation, and to eye the

Dred Scott case with a newly awakened interest. In *Prigg* the Court had said,

the cause has been brought here by the cooperation and sanction, both of the state of Maryland, and the state of Pennsylvania . . . so that the agitation on this subject, in both states, which has had a tendency to interrupt the harmony between them, may subside, and the conflict of opinion put to rest.

If the Court were to rule that Congress had no power to ban slavery in the territories, would that not, asked the slaveholders, "put to rest the conflict of opinion" that was tearing the country apart? And—again, just as *Prigg* paved the way for the Fugitive Slave Act of 1850— might not such a decision pave the way for direct federal intervention to protect the rights of slaveholders in the territories?

In November 1856 the presidential elections resulted in a victory for James Buchanan of Pennsylvania, the Democratic candidate who, along with his party, was deeply committed to the expansion of slavery into Kansas. Buchanan applied massive pressure to the Court to hand down a proslavery decision in the *Dred Scott* case. The Court was dominated by southerners; Chief Justice Roger B. Taney himself came from a Maryland slaveholding family. He wrote the decision for the Court in February 1857. On March 4 Buchanan was inaugurated. In his address he referred to the decision that was soon to be announced, and urged his countrymen to obey it. "To this decision," he said, "I shall cheerfully submit. . . . May we not, then, hope that the long agitation on this subject is approaching its end. Most happy will it be for the country when the public mind shall be diverted from this question to others of more pressing and practical importance."

The *Dred Scott* decision was handed down two days later, on March 6, 1857. We may characterize it as one of the most important decisions ever fashioned by an American court. It would take four years of war, torrents of blood, and a constitutional amendment to reverse it.

Mr. Justice Taney first of all addressed himself to the question of the jurisdiction of the federal courts, or their authority to hear and decide cases in which black people were parties to the suit. Does a black man, he asked, even if free, possess citizenship rights that would entitle him to sue in the federal courts? "Can a negro," he asked,

whose ancestors were imported into this country, and sold as slaves, become a member of the political community formed and brought into being by the Constitution of the United States, and as such become entitled to all the rights, privileges, and immunities, guaranteed by that instrument to the citizen, one of which rights is the privilege of suing in a court of the United States . . . ?

Taney's answer was no. The United States Circuit Court for the Missouri District ought to have refused to hear Scott's case. Scott simply had no *standing* in a federal court, that is, no right to come before it as a suitor for his rights.

Black people, Taney explained, had no right to the protection of the national courts, because they were not American "nationals," or citizens. When the founding fathers drew up the Constitution, he said, they had no

Chief Justice Roger B. Taney.

intention that it should protect the rights of black people as human beings or citizens. On the contrary; when the Constitution was created blacks were

considered as a subordinate and inferior class of beings, who had been subjugated by the dominant race, and, whether emancipated or not, yet remained subject to their authority, and had no rights or privileges but such as those who held the power and the Government might choose to grant them.

This argument we have encountered before. It was the colonizationist plea that blacks, as inferior beings, could never be admitted into the American community as full and equal members. Taney called this "an axiom in morals and politics." National citizenship, he said, was for whites only, for their children, and for other whites whom the federal government might choose to naturalize. Blacks were American "subjects," and it made no difference whether they were slave or free. They could never claim the protection of the American Constitution; they must be content with whatever rights the state governments, at their discretion, might confer upon them. In the eyes of the federal law, black people were not people at all; they were things.

Taney had now made a basic distinction between white citizen and black native, he had claimed lack of federal jurisdiction, and he had presumed to label the decision of the lower federal court in hearing the case a grievous error. He might now have directed that the case be sent back to the Supreme Court of the state of Missouri for final disposition. But he was only half done. If the federal government was obliged to enforce the Bill of

Rights for white people but not for black, what would follow? The Fifth Amendment states that no *person* shall "be deprived of life, liberty or property without due process of law." If blacks are defined as *things*, not persons, then this clause could only have one meaning: the federal government might not pass laws to deprive white people of the use of their property, including slaves. Laws such as the Missouri Compromise, banning slavery, amounted to unconstitutional confiscation of the property rights of white citizens. "An Act of Congress," said Taney, "which deprives a citizen of the United States of his liberty or property, merely because he came himself or brought his property into a particular territory . . . could hardly be identified with the name of due process."

Congress, in other words, could not bar slavery from the federal territories, because that would be meddling with the property rights of American citizens. With one clean cut, Taney threw open *all* the territories to slavery. Slavery, then, was national law, the law of the Constitution and the law of the land; and it had the right to go wherever the American flag might fly.

Northerners, thought Taney, must accept this fact. James Buchanan was confident that they would. In February 1858 he sent the proslavery constitution adopted by the proslavery party in Kansas—known as the Lecompton Constitution—to Congress with a message strongly advising Congress to accept and approve it. The basis for a proslavery constitution in Kansas, he pointed out, was the Supreme Court decision in the *Dred Scott* case. "It has," he wrote,

been solemnly adjudged, by the highest judicial tribunal

known to our laws, that slavery exists in Kansas by virtue of the Constitution of the United States; Kansas is, therefore, at this moment, as much a slave state as Georgia or South Carolina.

Such was the ultimatum of a southern-dominated Court to the free-state majority: Accept the rule of slavery and the law of slavery as national law and as constitutional principle.

Would the American people accept the Court's decision? What would happen if they did not?

THE MULTITUDINOUS SEAS
Abraham Lincoln and John Brown, 1858–1860

No; this my hand will rather
The multitudinous seas incarnadine,
Making the green one red.

Macbeth

It was 1858, only two years from the presidential elections of 1860, and the country was in a tumult over the *Dred Scott* decision and the struggle still being waged as to whether Kansas should be admitted to the Union as free or slave. Would northerners vote for another Democrat like Buchanan, who approved of and stood in back of the *Dred Scott* decision? Clearly, and for the first time in American history, the key issue in the national elections, the issue that would decide who won, would be the slavery question. The people were going to be called upon, as Abraham Lincoln used to put it, "to vote slavery up or down."

Southern Democrats, clearly enough, would have little problem in the elections; they would obviously try to nominate, and vote for, a Democrat who would run upon the *Dred Scott* decision. But for northerners it would be a different matter. What position *would* they take on slavery in the forthcoming elections?

The passage of the Kansas-Nebraska Act called forth, throughout the North, a movement of mass protest. This took the form not only of supporting the free-soil and free-settler movement in Kansas, but of forming a new party, the Republican party. It was a northern party and was organized state by state. The first state convention was held in Michigan, July 6, 1854, and was a group who came together in response to a "call" signed by over 10,000 Michigan people. Similar conventions were held the same month in Vermont, Ohio, Wisconsin, and Massachusetts. In every case there was really only one point on the program that the conventions discussed and voted: no more concessions to slaveholders, no more free territories to be signed away for slavery settlement.

The antislavery program of the Republicans was a minimal one that the greatest possible number of northerners might without difficulty be able to agree upon. The Republican program, in essence, reaffirmed the demand of the Wilmot Proviso that slavery be barred from all federal territories.

The birth of the Republican party marked the emergence of moderate, or conservative, antislavery politics as a major force in American life. It is necessary to distinguish carefully between the moderate antislavery people and the more radical abolitionists like William Lloyd Garrison, James G. Birney, and Theodore Weld. The moderates were opposed, first and foremost, to the expansion of slavery; they wished to put a stop to any further outward movement of the slavery system into

Republican campaign poster, 1856.

the federal territories. Moderates might deplore the sufferings of slaves, but they did not have any special concern for the rights of black people. On the contrary; moderates more often than not were colonizationists who believed that black people should be shipped out of the country as soon as practicable after they were emancipated. Their fear and hatred of slavery arose out of the fact that it was an always expanding social system which threatened to paralyze the growth of the free enterprise system then developing so rapidly throughout the North.

Harriet Stowe was one person who expressed to perfection the feelings of millions of moderate Republicans; another, as will be seen in a little while, was Abraham Lincoln.

The elections of 1856 speeded up the formation of the Republican party. Antislavery people from the Democratic and Whig parties flocked to it. The presidential candidate whom the Republicans nominated was John C. Fremont, a southerner who had won fame as an explorer of the West and as a military leader in the conquest of California from the Mexicans. The Republicans, evidently, were not against southerners, and they were not against the expansion of the United States. All they were against was the further expansion of the system of slavery.

The Republicans did not win the 1856 presidential election, but they made an impressive score, polling 1.3 million popular votes for Fremont against 1.8 million for Buchanan. The Whig party disappeared in these elections. In a flash the Republican party was a third party no longer; it was now the major opposition to the Democrats.

The shape of things to come in the elections of 1860 began to emerge in terms of the choices confronting the American people. The Republican program had simplicity and directness. But the Democrats were split. Southern Democrats, as might be expected, would want a candidate who would stand squarely behind the *Dred Scott* decision. For northern Democrats and their leader, Stephen Douglas, *Dred Scott* presented problems. In the first place, most northerners—and northern voters were the majority—simply wouldn't buy it. In the second place, *Dred Scott*, which claimed the slaveholder's *right* to the territories, collided squarely with Douglas's own position, that territorial settlers could exclude slavery if they chose. As between a Republican candidate barring the door to slavery in the territories and a Democratic candidate supporting popular sovereignty, which would most northerners choose?

In 1858, the North was given a very important trial run on this question. Senator Douglas was up for re-election in Illinois as a candidate for the United States Senate; and the Republicans put their leading Illinois man, Abraham Lincoln, in the race against him. The Illinois correspondent of the *New York Semi-Weekly Post* described the Republican senatorial candidate as follows:

A native of Kentucky, where he belonged to the class of "poor whites," he came early to Illinois. Poor, unfriended, uneducated, a day-laborer, he has distanced all these disadvantages, and in the profession of the law he has risen steadily to a competence, and to the position of an intelligent, shrewd, and well-balanced man. Familiarly known as "Long Abe," he is a popular speaker *and a cautious, thoughtful politician capable of taking a high position as a statesman and legislator.*

Lincoln challenged Douglas to a series of public debates to be held in different towns throughout the state of Illinois. In these debates, the rival doctrines of popular sovereignty and "free soil" were to be explained, challenged, and defended before large audiences.

Here is the challenge that Lincoln sent to Senator Douglas on July 24, 1858:

My Dear Sir: Will it be agreeable to you to make an arrangement for you and myself to divide time, and address the same audiences [during] the present canvass. Mr. Judd [Chairman of the Republican State Central Committee] is authorized to receive your answer and, if agreeable to you, to enter into the terms of such agreement. Your obedient servant, A. Lincoln.

In his reply, Douglas suggested that there might be seven debates in seven different towns throughout the state. And so it was agreed. The first six debates were held at Ottawa, Freeport, Jonesboro, Charleston, Galesburg, and Quincy, between August 21 and October 13. The last of the series was held at Alton, October 15, in front of the new City Hall, and only a stone's throw from the river bluff where Elijah Lovejoy had been buried twenty-one years before.

These debates are known to history as the Lincoln-Douglas Debates. Their national importance was instantly recognized: by defining the issues facing the northern electorate in the forthcoming elections of 1860, the debates would shape the future of the party system, and they would help decide the fate of the country itself.

These were the first political speeches ever to be recorded in shorthand by correspondents who traveled with the candidates. Stands, gaily decked with flags, were put up in the public squares. Lincoln and Douglas, with only the strength of their own unaided voices and the power of their own lungs to sustain them, spoke in the open air to audiences estimated to run as high as ten thousand people. Here is the scene at the opening debate at Ottawa, as described by the *Chicago Press and Tribune*:

From sunrise till high noon Ottawa was deluged in dust. The first of the seven great debates which Douglas had consented to hold with Lincoln had started . . . the surrounding counties, in [to] unwonted commotion. Before breakfast Ottawa was beleaguered with a multiplying host from all points of the compass. . . . Teams, trains, and processions poured in from every direction like an army with banners. National flags, mottoes, and devices fluttered and stared from every street corner. Military companies and bands of music monopolized the thoroughfares around the court house and the public square.

And so throughout the late summer and early fall, Lincoln and Douglas moved around the state, talking, at the top of their lungs, from dusty, sun-scorched platforms to huge and sweating audiences. There was, naturally, much repetition in what both men said as they moved from place to place. Douglas, for his part, hammered home at the theme that the Republican party was a sectional organization, that it was appealing only to the North, that it was dividing the country.

That party is unlike all other political organizations in this country. All other parties have been national in their

Stephen Douglas.

character, have avowed their principles alike in the slave and the free states. . . . But now you have a sectional organization, a party which speaks to the Northern section of the Union against the Southern, a party which appeals to Northern passion, Northern pride, Northern ambition, against Southern people, the Southern states, and Southern institutions. The leaders of that party hope that they will be able to unite the Northern states into one great sectional party . . . that they will thus be enabled to outvote, conquer, govern, and control the South.

Douglas went on to make the serious charge that Lincoln was an abolitionist. In one place, said Douglas, Lincoln

took the ground that the Negro race is included in the Declaration of Independence as the equal of the white race, and that there could be no such thing as a distinction in the races, making one superior and the other inferior.

At another place, in order to get the votes of moderates, Lincoln concealed his real views, Douglas charged, and preached the superiority of the white race. Lincoln said,

I will say that there is a physical difference between the white and the black races which, I suppose, will forever forbid the two races living together upon terms of social and political equality; and inasmuch as they cannot so live, while they do remain together I, as much as any other man, am in favor of the superior position being assigned to the white man.

As for himself, said Douglas, he scorned to hide his views about black people; his position was the same as

Justice Taney's. It was heresy to say, as Lincoln had said, that black and white people ought to enjoy equal rights. The signers of the Declaration of Independence

never dreamed of the Negro when they were writing that document. They referred to white men, to men of Euro-pean birth and European descent when they declared the equality of all men. I see a gentleman there in the crowd shaking his head. Let me remind him that when Thomas Jefferson wrote that document, he was the owner, and so continued until his death, of a large number of slaves. Did he intend to say in the Declaration that his Negro slaves, which he held and treated as property, were created his equals by divine law, and that he was violating the law of God every day of his life by holding them as slaves?

Douglas went on to answer his own question. He aligned himself bluntly with the extremist views of the southern slaveholders:

I say to you frankly that in my opinion this government was made by our fathers on the white basis. It was made by white men for the benefit of white men and their posterity forever, and was intended to be administered by white men in all time to come.

Douglas went on to defend the right of whites in the territories to choose slavery if they pleased; and he tried to reconcile this, as best he could, with the *Dred Scott* decision: "Mr. Lincoln cannot be made to understand how it is that in a territory the people can do as they please on the slavery question." Douglas argued that the local settlers had a right, if they chose, to pass legislation "unfriendly" to slavery, which would make this form of property worthless. Let us assume a slaveholder traveling to an "unfriendly" territory: "When he gets his slaves there," said Douglas,

he finds that there is no local law to protect him in holding them, no slave code, no police regulation maintaining him in his right, and he discovers at once that the absence of such friendly legislation excludes his property from the territory just as irresistibly as if there was a positive constitutional prohibition excluding it.

Douglas summed up his position on popular sovereignty as follows: "The great fundamental principle of our government "is that the people of each state and territory shall be left perfectly free to decide for themselves what shall be the nature and character of their institutions."

Abraham Lincoln spoke on behalf of the Republican party and explained its position with regard to slavery. There was nothing outwardly remarkable about this man now making a reputation for himself for the beauty, power, and simplicity of his public speaking. An observer at the time recalled that,

His clothes hung awkwardly upon his giant frame; his face was of a dark pallor without the slightest tinge of color; his seamed and rugged features bore the furrows of hardship and struggle; his deep-set eyes looked sad and anxious.

In each debate Lincoln lost no time coming to grips with Douglas's position that the Declaration of Independence, when it talked of the right to liberty, had no reference to black Americans; that it was a matter of indifference whether a black man was slave or free. "The Judge," said Lincoln,

has alluded to the Declaration of Independence and insisted that Negroes are not included in the Declaration; and that it is a slander upon the framers of that instrument to suppose that Negroes were meant therein. . . . I will remind Judge Douglas and this audience that while Mr. Jefferson was the owner of slaves, as undoubtedly he was, in speaking upon this very subject, he used the strong language that "he trembled for his country when he remembered that God was just"; and I will offer the highest premium in my power to Judge Douglas if he will show that he, in all his life, ever uttered a sentiment at all akin to that of Jefferson.

Lincoln, then, believed that all men are equal, that they have a right to life, liberty, and happiness. But, he said, it did not follow that he would urge the abolition of inequalities in the North out of hand, or that he would advocate the immediate abolition of slavery in the South. Not at all. "I have never," he said,

manifested any impatience with the necessities that spring from the actual presence of black people amongst us, and the actual existence of slavery amongst us where it does already exist; but I have insisted that, in legislating for new countries where it does not exist, there is no just rule other than of moral and abstract right!

In these words, Lincoln defined very carefully the position he took on the question of slavery and black people. He was not "impatient" with the wrongs that

Abraham Lincoln, from an 1860 photograph.

black people endured both in the North and the South. As we know from other of his writings, Lincoln's position was close to that of the colonizationists. Black people, certainly, had rights under the Declaration of Independence, just as the rights of all mankind were recognized in that document. But those rights must be exercized in Africa or, at any event, beyond the borders of the United States. Lincoln differed with Douglas on one apparently small but nonetheless crucial point. Slavery, as the Declaration said and as Jefferson agreed, was *wrong*. If it was wrong, then its wrongness could not be a matter of indifference either to the American people or their government. An institution that was wrong could not be permitted to spread to new lands, to root itself in new territories won by purchase or conquest. Such a thing violated the spirit of the Constitution which was expressed for all time in the Declaration.

Abraham Lincoln, as we see, was not very far from the "conservative abolitionism" of Harriet Beecher Stowe. His position, we might even say, was the political expression of the moral insight which, in the *Cabin*, she had popularized among millions. Everything that Douglas said, Lincoln explained, or that his friends said,

excludes the thought that there is anything wrong in slavery. All their arguments, if you will consider them, will be seen to exclude the thought that there is anything whatever wrong in slavery. If you will take the Judge's speeches and select the sharp and pointed sentences expressed by him—as his declaration that he "don't care whether slavery is voted up or down"—you will see at once that this is perfectly logical, if you do not admit that slavery is wrong. If you do admit that it is wrong, Judge Douglas cannot logically say he don't care whether a wrong is voted up or down.

Judge Douglas declares that if any community wants slavery, they have a right to it. He can say that logically, if he says that there is no wrong in slavery; but if you admit that there is a wrong in it, he cannot say logically that anybody has a right to do wrong.

This, Lincoln concluded, was the essential difference between Douglas and himself. Douglas and his friends did not care if slavery kept on growing, expanding; Lincoln and the Republicans did. They thought slavery was wrong and must therefore be brought to an end. They wished to shape a national policy "that looks to the prevention of slavery as a wrong and looks hopefully to the time when as a wrong it may come to an end."

Lincoln turned, next, to Douglas's doctrine of popular sovereignty and the *Dred Scott* decision. He had little difficulty in showing that the two positions were totally in conflict with each other. Taney had held, said Lincoln, that a slaveholder's right to hold slaves in the federal territories was explicitly sanctioned by the Constitution. How then could *any* territorial laws or regulations defeating that right be anything but a defiance of federal law?

Douglas, said Lincoln, was obviously illogical in his position, but he was nonetheless giving vast aid to the slavery cause. With a pose of moral indifference—"saying he don't care whether slavery is voted up or down"—he was blunting popular opposition to its ominous, inexorable advance. "If," said he,

Judge Douglas's policy upon this question succeeds and gets fairly settled down, until all opposition is crushed out, the next thing will be a grab for the territory of poor Mexico, an invasion of the rich lands of South America, then the adjoining islands will follow, each one of which promises additional slave-fields.

Now he came to the climax of his harsh and memorable attack. "I do think," said he,

that Judge Douglas and whoever like him teaches that the Negro has no share, humble though it may be, in the Declaration of Independence, is going back to the era of our liberty and independence and, so far as in him lies, muzzling the cannon that thunders its annual joyous return; that he is blowing out the moral lights around us, when he contends that whoever wants slaves has a right to hold them; that he is penetrating, so far as lies in his power, the human soul, and eradicating the light of reason and the love of liberty when he is in every possible way preparing the public mind, by his vast influence, for making the institution of slavery perpetual and national.

Abraham Lincoln did not win the Illinois election, but the debates made him a national figure. Invitations began to arrive from all over the country, urging him to visit and to lecture.

On October 17, 1859, just one year after the Alton debate, Lincoln was at home in Springfield, working on a talk that he had been asked to give in New York City. As he wrote, the stunning news arrived that twenty-two men had seized the federal arsenal at Harper's Ferry in West Virginia and had tried to begin a general rising of the slaves.

John Brown, the leader of this band, was born in 1800 in Torrington, Connecticut, a descendant of Peter Brown, who came over to this country on the *Mayflower*. Brown, in the course of a busy life, followed many trades —tanner, businessman, wool dealer, cattle breeder, and farmer. As the years went by, he pondered deeply about slavery and began to dream about the liberation of the slaves. In 1834, he was turning over the idea of starting a school for black youth. "If the young blacks of our country," he wrote his brother, "could once become enlightened, it would most assuredly operate on slavery like firing powder confined in a rock, and all slave-holders know it well."

At some point Brown concluded, even as Nat Turner before him, that he was God's chosen instrument to accomplish the freedom of the slaves. This objective became the ruling passion of his life. Unlike Turner, Brown was educated and could read what he chose. He studied the history of previous slave uprisings—in the provinces of the Roman Empire, on the French island of Haiti— and formed a bold and revolutionary plan. He would raise his standard in the mountains; he would make his base in the Appalachian chain running from Virginia to Alabama and plunging, like a dagger, into the very heart of the South. Together his abolitionist band and the slaves who flocked to him would form a military striking force and the foundation of a free southern state. "If any hostility," Brown explained to Richard Realf in 1858,

were taken against us, either by the militia of the states or by the armies of the United States, we purpose to defeat first the militia and next, if possible, the troops of the United States; and then organize the free blacks

Beginning of John Brown's trial, Charlestown, Va., 1859.

under the provisional constitution, which would carve
out for the locality of its jurisdiction all that mountainous
region in which the blacks were to be established. . . .

In 1855, Brown emigrated to Kansas with his sons and
took part in the bloody civil war that raged there until
1856. He returned to the East in 1857. In 1859 he decided that his time had come. In the summer of that
year he gathered together a small striking force on a farm
not far from the Federal Arsenal at Harper's Ferry in
West Virginia.

Brown possessed the qualities of a charismatic leader.
He was, in this, the last year of his life, described by a
contemporary witness as follows:

He stooped somewhat as he walked, was rather narrow shouldered. Went looking on the ground almost all the time, with his head bent forward apparently in study or thought. Walked rather rapidly and very energetically. His features were very sharp, nose prominent, eyes were black or very dark grey.

Brown and his party stole into Harper's Ferry in the dark of night late Sunday, October 16, and seized the armory. Then they began to capture slaveholders and to liberate their slaves.

But no uprising of the slaves took place, if that was what Brown expected. By early afternoon of October 17, Virginia militia began to arrive and to attack the armory. Brown and his followers were dislodged from one building but kept control of an engine house. Late that night, the U.S. Marines arrived and were placed under the command of Colonel Robert E. Lee. The following morning, federal troops stormed Brown's refuge and took it. Brown with four others was made prisoner. He was badly wounded, suffering several sword and bayonet thrusts. All the rest of his band was dead, wounded, or missing. Oliver and Watson, two of Brown's sons, were dead. Another son, John, had already been killed in 1855 in Kansas in the struggle against slave settlers at Osawatomi.

The state of Virginia lost no time in trying Brown for rebellion, treason, and murder. The indictment was handed down on October 26 at Charlestown, Jefferson County, against Brown, Aaron Stephens, Edwin Coppie, Shields Green, and John Copland. Stephens and Coppie were white; Green and Copland, black. The second count of this indictment charged that the five did conspire:

to induce certain slaves . . . and other slaves to the jurors unknown, to rebel and make insurrection against their masters and owners, and against the Government and the Constitution and laws of the Commonwealth of Virginia . . . .

On Monday, October 31, John Brown was found guilty, and two days later was sentenced to hang. Before sentence of death was passed, he rose from the bed upon which he had lain during the trial, and addressed the court. "I see a book kissed," he said,

which I suppose to be the Bible, or at least the New Testament, which teaches me that all things whatsoever I would that men should do to me, I should do even so to them. It teaches me to remember them that are in bonds as bound with them. I endeavored to act up to that instruction. . . . I believe that to have interfered as I have done, as I have always freely admitted I have done in behalf of His despised poor, is no wrong, but right. Now, if it is deemed necessary that I should forfeit my life for the furtherance of the ends of justice and mingle my blood further with the blood of my children and with the blood of millions in this slave country, whose rights are disregarded by wicked, cruel, and unjust enactments, I say let it be done.

One month later the old man was led out from the jail and taken to the gallows. His coffin was placed in a wagon, and he sat down upon it, alongside of the jailer, Captain Avis. The wagon with its military escort was then drawn away to the place of execution. "This is a beautiful country," said Brown to Captain Avis as they moved along, "I have never had the pleasure of seeing it before."

December 3, and John Brown was no more. Abraham Lincoln placed the finishing touches to his speech and traveled east to deliver it before a distinguished audience at Cooper Union in Manhattan, February 1860. John Brown's raid, he told the people, was absurd; the old man, he said, was "an enthusiast brooding over the oppression of a people till he fancies himself commissioned by Heaven to liberate them. He ventures the attempt, which ends up in little else than his own execution."

The Republican party was impressed with Lincoln; he was a fine speaker, he was a moderate, and he came from the Midwest. They nominated him as their candidate for President, and he won the election in November. This election triggered the Civil War, for it marked the organization of the antislavery majority into a *bloc* prepared to use the federal power to prevent any further territorial expansion of the slavery system.

South Carolina was the first state to secede from the Union in December 1860. By April 1861 most of the southern states had trooped out after her and had formed a government of their own, the Confederate States of America. Four years of struggle against slavery were about to begin; they would cost the nation more than half a million lives and end with the surrender of the southern army at Appomattox in April 1865. Two years earlier, on January 1, 1863, Abraham Lincoln had issued a wartime proclamation declaring that the slaves were free. Like John Brown, he paid for his deed with his life.

John Brown of Massachusetts

Guitar   CV   CIII   Old

John Brown's bo - dy is   a-mould- e - ring in the dust, Old

John Brown's rif - le's red with blood spots turned to rust, Old

John Brown's pike has made its last, un - flinch- ing thrust, His

soul is march - ing on!

Chorus

Glo - ry glo - ry Hal - le - lu - jah,

"For - ward!" calls the Lord, our Cap - tain:

Glo - ry, glo - ry Hal - le - lu - jah, With

him we're march - ing on.

For treason hung because he struck at treason's root,
When soon palmetto-tree had ripened treason's fruit,
His dust, disquieted, stirred at Sumter's last salute –
His soul is marching on.

Glory glory Hallelujah,
"Forward!" calls the Lord, our Captain:
Glory, glory Hallelujah,
With him we're marching on.

Who rides before the army of martyrs to the word?
The heavens grow bright as He makes bare his flaming sword,
The glory fills the earth of the coming of the Lord,
His soul is marching on.

CHORUS

His sacrifice we share! Our sword shall victory crown!
For God and country strike the fiend Rebellion down!
For freedom and the right remember old John Brown!
His soul is marching on!

CHORUS

THE FRUITFUL BOUGH
Epilogue

Joseph is a fruitful bough,
Even a fruitful bough by a well;
Whose branches run over the wall:
The archers have sorely grieved him,
And shot at him, and hated him:
But his bow abode in strength
And the arms of his hands were made strong
By the hands of the mighty God of Jacob.

Book of Genesis

The Thirteenth Amendment decreeing the abolition of slavery became a part of the American Constitution in 1865. "Neither slavery nor involuntary servitude," it said, "shall exist within the United States, or any place subject to their jurisdiction." Congress, it added, was empowered to enforce this decree "by appropriate legislation."

Without too much fear of contradiction, the Thirteenth Amendment may be called the most revolutionary article in the Constitution. It conferred upon Congress a virtually limitless power to root up slavery and to blot it out. This new national power would be limited only by the nation's understanding of what slavery was—by its definition of the *concept* of slavery.

How then, is this crucial concept of slavery to be defined; and who is to do the defining?

A definition of slavery is not something that men or women can make up out of their own heads, to suit their own convenience. History alone, the sum total of the American experience, is capable of writing out that definition. Slavery was an historical reality; what it was can be illuminated by historical study alone. Some elements of this reality have emerged in the foregoing pages, and they have been defined from the lips of the people who endured the slavery experience and were, therefore, best qualified to speak about it.

Slavery, Kenneth Stampp has said, "was above all a labor system." Certainly, slavery was a labor system, but it was also more than that. As Harriet Beecher Stowe saw with such clarity, slavery was above all an entire social system. Through ownership of the broad plantations of the South and of the people who toiled upon those plantations, the slave owners were able to impose their will upon millions of their less affluent white fellow citizens.

Slavery was sustained not alone by force but also by the power of ideas. The philosophy of slavery, which was expounded by George McDuffie and dozens of southern writers and intellectuals, taught the superiority of the white race, the inferiority of blacks, and the right of the master race to use black people, and if necessary destroy them, in the pursuit of private interest and profit.

The fact of ownership and exploitation found an important but considerably narrower expression in law. It is right and proper, said the law, for some people to own others, to buy and sell them, to pass them on to their heirs. It is right and proper, said the law, to pursue a slave if he flees; and to drag him back with aid of chains, whips, dogs, and guns.

In order to succeed in its objective of forcing labor out of black people, slavery was obliged to deny movement to the slaves, not only in terms of flight, but also by forcing slaves to be, *at all times*, where they were supposed to be—by day in the fields, by night in the huts. This denial of the right of movement, this freezing to a single spot, was accomplished by a system of overseers, drivers, patrols, and the lash. It was compulsory segregation—and this is exactly what segregation means: it is the act of cutting one group off from others and compelling it to exist in isolation. Without segregation slavery could not have hoped to survive for a single day; it was basic both to the labor system and to the society.

Philosophy and law gave the white man the authority and the power to destroy the slave, to lash him, to maim him, to blot him out if he dared offer resistance to the system and to the atrocious violence that it inflicted upon him. Slavery defended its supremacy against the tide of black revolt by use of the ultimate sanctions of punishment and death. Slavery, therefore, was genocidal. It claimed the right to break human beings or to destroy them simply because they were black.

Black people, Taney ruled in *Dred Scott*, were American *subjects*; it did not matter to him whether they were slaves or "free." Black people, so Taney ruled, could never be fully or truly free in the United States. This exclusion, he ruled, was based on *color*, nothing else.

Precisely because color was used as the basis for exclusion, it pressed black people into a common mold and endowed them with a common historical experience; an experience they all shared, because they were black, but that nobody else shared, because they were not.

Segregation meant a separate existence which, over the course of time, created a separate black nationality, a people bound together by memories of the African past and by an American reality the like of which no other immigrant group ever experienced or endured. All this was sealed by a common struggle against the oppressor; and by a common Protestant religion that taught the equality of all believers and a common destiny for all black people—to be freed from the Pharaohs and to find the Promised Land. Out of this black nationality has come a song, a legend, and a literature that has enriched American culture and that has, at the same time, been a contribution to humanity itself.

In this respect the experience of the black people was the opposite of all other ethnic groups. Other immigrant peoples were encouraged, indeed compelled, to relinquish their ethnic identity as a condition of acceptance into American society. This violent shearing away of ethnic traditions and life styles was politely termed "assimilation." But the black people were not permitted to assimilate; in the long years of separate existence they created a new Afro-American culture as a condition of struggle, identity, survival.

The struggle against slavery was initiated by the black people themselves—by Denmark Vesey, Nat Turner, Harriet Tubman, Henry Bibb, Frederick Douglass, Solomon Northup, and the countless thousands of men, women, and children who endured bondage and found their own ways to protest against it.

In the course of time white people, too, became involved in the struggle against slavery as a social system. In a general sense two streams in this struggle are to be distinguished. Moderates, on the one side, saw slavery primarily as an expanding empire that threatened to engulf the Union and paralyze the growth of the free-enterprise, free-labor system that prevailed throughout the North. When the military power of the slaveholders and the expansive power of the slavery system was destroyed in the Civil War, the moderates relaxed and breathed more easily. With the supremacy of the Union over all its territories re-established, they were content to accept the abolition of *one aspect* of slavery only: the legal ownership of man by man.

Radical abolitionists were concerned with much more than this. They saw that the struggle against slavery could never end until black people had won total freedom—that is, an equal place with whites in American society. Some black abolitionists realized that this could not happen until blacks had liberated themselves from the tremendous psychological burden imposed upon them by the long years of enforced separation. In a much broader sense, the abolitionist dream is part of the rainbow-hued vision of social justice in a land that has been promised to the American people but that is not yet totally theirs. This is a dream that belongs to the future as much as to the past.

SONG NOTES

All guitar accompaniments copyright by John Anthony Scott

Lay This Body Down is a lament and funeral song from the Georgia and Carolina Sea Islands. It is perhaps one of the most moving songs that we have inherited from slavery days.

Hushabye served at one and the same time as a lullabye for white babies and a lament for black ones. Women slaves cradled the master's children, or worked in the fields, while their own lay unwatched and uncared for.

Long Summer Day was collected by Alan Lomax in south Texas. Lomax describes this song as "one of the few authentic slave work songs, text and tune, that have been found anywhere."

I Sought My Lord is a slave work-song from the Sea Islands, and a re-creation, by black people, of a popular white spiritual, *Out of the Wilderness*.

Oh Freedom: We know little about the precise origins of this spiritual, and it may not be much older than the time of the Civil War: but it comes down to us as the greatest of the 19th century American freedom songs.

Hangman is a variant of a very old English song, *The Sycamore Tree*. It is one of many British ballads that were loved and sung by black people throughout the South during slavery. This particular version of the song is from Florida.

Poor Rosy was, at one and the same time, a spiritual, a love song, a work song, and a lament. A great favorite among Sea Island slaves, it captures in an unrivaled way the human meaning of slavery and its ultimate sorrow.

Michael is a Sea Island spiritual and work song that was "discovered" by singers in the 1950's and which has re-entered our singing tradition of recent years.

John Brown of Massachusetts is a Civil War marching song whose lyrics, as given here, were very popular with Massachusetts soldiers.

ACKNOWLEDGMENTS

Elizabeth Jannot helped with a perceptive reading of original sources. Rachel Ginzberg and Maria Scott read the manuscript chapter by chapter and offered creative suggestions. Rod Harrison and Arthur Kinoy discussed with me the meaning of slavery and provided new insights; they are only two of many students and colleagues who, over the years, have done the same. Elizabeth Urbanowicz prepared successive drafts with speed, patience, and inspiration. Elizabeth Phillips saw the book through the press and was a model editor.

Grateful acknowledgment is made for the use of illustrations:

Pennsylvania Academy of the Fine Arts, bequest of Henry C. Carey, 9; New York Public Library Picture Collection, 14, 24, 33, 37, 43, 62, 91, 196, 212, 223; The New York Historical Society, 56, 134; Library of Congress, 81, 82, 169, 239, 250, 255, 260; New York Public Library, 59, 94, 101, 113, 118, 123, 147, 160, 199, 207; The Granger Collection, 103, 185, 234, 245; The Metropolitan Museum of Art, Gift of I. N. Phelps Stokes, Edward S. Hawes, Alice Mary Hawes, Marion Augusta Hawes, 1937, 131, 204; The Stowe-Day Foundation, 153.

BIBLIOGRAPHY

This bibliography has been designed for the reference of teachers, students, and school librarians. It includes the main sources used in the preparation of this book, and offers suggestions for further reading on the various topics. All works listed are in print at the time of writing (1974) unless otherwise stated.

General

In the 1930's, ex-slaves' recollections of slavery were taken down under the auspices of the Federal Writers' Project of the Works Progress Administration. This archive has been published by Greenwood Publishing Co. (Westport, Conn.: 1972, 19 vols.) under the title of *The American Slave: A Composite Autobiography*. This record is of uneven quality, but it is indispensable for the study of American slavery. A helpful commentary on the archive is provided by the general editor, George P. Rawick, in vol. 1 of the series: *From Sundown to Sunup: The Making of the Black Community*. See also the brilliantly chosen selections of Norman R. Yetman, ed., *Voices from Slavery* (New York: Holt, Rinehart and Winston, 1970; hardcover and paperback); and Julius Lester, *To Be A Slave* (New York: Dial Press, 1968; hardcover and paperback).

A number of the writings of slaves or ex-slaves have been reissued recently, and these are also of the greatest value for the study of the institution of slavery and the battle against it, notably: Solomon Northup, *Twelve Years A Slave* (Baton Rouge: Louisiana University Press, 1969, eds. Sue Eakin and Joseph Logsdon; also a Dover Publications paperback); Josiah Henson, *Father Henson's Story of His Own Life* (1858. Reissued by Corner House Publishers, Williamstown, Mass., 1973; Corinth Books paperback, 1962); *A Narrative of the Life and Adventures of Henry Bibb, An American Slave, Written by Himself* (1850. Reissued by Negro Universities Press, New York; 1969); Frederick Douglass, *Narrative of the Life of an American Slave* (Harvard, Mass.: The Belknap Press, 1960); Charles Ball, *Fifty Years in Chains* (1836. Reissued by Dover Publications, Inc., New York: 1970); and Anne Griffiths, *The Autobiography of a Female Slave* (1857. Reissued by Negro Universities Press, New York: 1969).

Plantation journals, records, and diaries are helpful in studying slavery, as are travelers' accounts. There is Thomas Jefferson's *Farm Book* in the superb edition prepared by Edwin Betts (Philadelphia: American Philosophic Society, 1953); John Blackford, *Ferry Hill Plantation Journal: Jan. 4, 1838 to January 15, 1839* (Chapel Hill, N.C.: University of North Carolina Press, 1961, ed. Fletcher M. Green); and Albert Virgil House, ed., *Planter Management and Capitalism in Ante-Bellum Georgia: The Journal of High Fraser Grant, Ricegrower* (New York: Columbia University Press, 1954). Frances A. Kemble, *Journal of a Residence on a Georgian Plantation in 1838–9* (1863. Reissued by Alfred A. Knopf, Inc., New York: 1961, ed. John Anthony Scott) is a unique account of plantation life. Mary Boykin Chesnut, *A Diary From Dixie*, Ben Ames Williams, ed., (Boston: Houghton Mifflin paperback, 1961) is a Civil War journal kept by the mistress of a Southern plantation, which tells a lot about the planter aristocracy and its way of life. Another very useful source of the same kind is Edmund Ruffin's *Diary* (Baton Rouge: Louisiana State University Press, 1971, ed. William Kauffman Scarborough). Among the numerous travelers' accounts, J. S. Buckingham, *The Slave States of America* (1836. Reissued by Negro Universities Press, New York: 1968), contains much vivid detail; Frederick Law Olmsted, *The Cotton*

Kingdom (1861. Reissued New York: Alfred A. Knopf, Inc., 1953, ed. Arthur M. Schlesinger) is a classic; see also the same author's *Journey in the Back Country* (1860. Reissued as a Schocken paperback, New York: 1970).

The records of the courts are a fundamental source for the study of the slave South. An indispensable reference in this area is Helen Catterall, ed., *Judicial Cases Concerning American Slavery*, 5 vols. (1926. Reissued by Negro Universities Press, New York: 1968). Useful commentary is provided by William Goodell, *The American Slave Code in Theory and Practice* (1853. Reissued by Johnson Reprint Corp., New York: 1968), and this may be supplemented by Harriet Beecher Stowe's unequalled analysis in Part II of *A Key to Uncle Tom's Cabin* (1853. Reissued by Arno Press, New York: 1968).

The struggle of black people to preserve elements of their African heritage and to create an Afro-American culture of their own is most poignantly and beautifully illustrated in the realm of religion, song, and dance. The pioneer study is Henry Edward Krehbiel, *Afro-American Folksongs: A Study in Racial and National Music* (1914. Reissued by Frederick Ungar Publishing Co., New York: 1962). The first great collection of slavery songs to appear was William Francis Allen, Charles Pickard Ware and Lucy McKim Garrison, *Slave Songs of the United States* (1867. Reissued by Peter Smith, Gloucester, Mass.: 1951). Among later collections of slave spirituals and songs, the following are outstanding: Dorothy Scarborough, *On the Trail of Negro Folk Songs* (1925. Reissued by Folklore Associates, Hatboro, Pennsylvania: 1963); Mary Allen Grissom, *The Negro Sings a New Heaven* (1930. Reissued by Dover Publications, New York: 1969); and Lydia Parrish, *Slave Songs of the Georgia Sea Islands* (1942. Reissued by Folklore Associates, Hatboro, Pennsylvania: 1965).

Available sources for the study of the abolitionist movement include: the letters of William Lloyd Garrison (Belknap Press of Harvard University Press), Theodore Weld, Angelina Grimke and Sarah Grimke (Da Capo Press), and James G. Birney (Peter Smith). Theodore Weld's famous *Slavery As It Is* is available (New York: Arno Press, 1968) and is also in an abridged version (Itasca, Illinois: F. E. Peacock Inc., 1972, ed. Curry and Dowden). For firsthand accounts of the underground railroad see Sojourner Truth, *Narrative* (1876. Reissued by Arno Press, New York: 1968); William Still, *The Underground Railroad* (1872 reissued by Arno Press, 1968); and Levi Coffin, *Reminiscences* (1876. Reissued by Augustus Kelley, New York: 1968).

Turning to secondary sources, Kenneth Stampp, *The Peculiar Institution* (New York: Alfred A. Knopf, Inc., 1956; Vintage paperback) is an unequalled survey. Slavery ideology is examined in Clement Eaton, *The Mind of the Old South* (Baton Rouge: Louisiana State University Press, 1967), and John Hope Franklin, *The Militant South* (Cambridge, Mass.: Belknap Press, 1956). The life of Southern whites is examined in Roger W. Shugg, *Origins of Class Struggle in Louisiana: A Social History of White Farmers and Laborers During Slavery and After* (Baton Rouge: Louisiana State University Press, 1939, 1966), and Frank Owsley, *Plain Folk of the Old South* (1949. Reissued Chicago: Quadrangle paperback, 1965). Clement Eaton, *The Growth of Southern Civilization 1790–1860* (New York: Harper Torchbook, 1963), contains a wealth of descriptive material and a full bibliography.

For the history of the abolitionist movement, Benjamin Quarles, *Black Abolitionists* (New York: Oxford University Press, 1969) and Gerald Sorin, *Abolitionism, A New Perspective* (New York: Praeger Publisher, 1972; paperback) provide a condensed overview. For the underground railroad, see Wilbur H. Siebert, *The Underground Railroad from Slavery to Freedom* (1898. Reissued Peter Smith, Gloucester, Mass.: 1968); Horatio T. Strother, *The Underground Railroad in Connecticut* (Middletown, Conn.: Wesleyan University Press, 1962); and Larry Gara's critical study, *The Liberty Line: The Legend of the Underground Railroad* (Lexington: University of Kentucky Press, 1961; hardcover and paperback).

The rise of antislavery consciousness in the nation at large is dealt with in Elbert B. Smith, *The Death of Slavery: The United States 1837–65* (Chicago: University of Chicago Press, 1967), which also has a useful bibliographical guide. See also Eric

Foner, *Free Soil, Free Labor, Free Men: The Ideology of the Republican Party Before the Civil War* (New York: Oxford University Press, 1971; Galaxy paperback).

1/The Black Cloud

Pierce Butler's role in the Constitutional Convention of 1787 is recorded in detail in Max Farrand, ed., *The Records of the Federal Convention of 1787* (New Haven: Yale University Press, 4 vols., revised edition, 1937; hardcover and paperback). Fanny Kemble's account of the Butler plantations is given in *Journal of a Residence on a Georgian Plantation in 1838–1839*, cited above. For biographical detail see also John Anthony Scott, *Fanny Kemble's America* (New York: Thomas Y. Crowell Co., 1973).

2/New-Fallen Snow

A masterful survey of the Cotton Kingdom by a contemporary is Frederick Law Olmsted, *The Cotton Kingdom*, cited above. See also J. S. Buckingham, *The Slave States of America*, cited above. The definitive account of the internal slave trade is Frederic Bancroft, *Slave Trading in the Old South*, ed. Allan Nevins (1931. Reissued New York: Frederick Ungar Publishing Co., 1959). For the development of the cotton gin, see Jeannette Mirsky and Allan Nevins, *The World of Eli Whitney* (New York: Collier Books paperback, 1962).

3/Down in the Wilderness

For specific detail this chapter drew upon *The American Slave*, cited above, especially the Texas, Missouri, South Carolina, Georgia, and Oklahoma narratives. Also Frances Anne Kemble, *Journal of a Residence*, Frederick Law Olmsted, *Cotton Kingdom*, Frederick Douglass, *Narrative*, and Solomon Northup, *Twelve Years a Slave*, all cited above. See also Frantz Fanon, *The Wretched of the Earth* (1963. Translated from the French by Constance Farrington and issued by Grove Press, New York: 1966; Evergreen paperback).

4/Jesus Is Black

The Confessions of Nat Turner, the Leader of the Late Insurrection in Southampton, Va. were published by Thomas R. Gray as a pamphlet in Baltimore in 1831. The *Confessions* have been reissued by Harvey Wish, ed., in *Slavery in the South* (New York: Noonday Press paperback, 1964), and also as the Appendix of John Henrik Clarke ed., *William Styron's Nat Turner* (Boston: Beacon Press paperback, 1968). This book includes critical reviews by black writers of William Styron's, *The Confessions of Nat Turner* (New York: Random House, 1966; hardcover and paperback). The other great revolts of this period were those of Gabriel in Henrico County, Virginia (1800), and of Denmark Vesey in Charleston, South Carolina (1822). Gabriel is the subject of a fine study by Arna Bontemps, *Black Thunder* (1936. Reissued as a Beacon paperback, Boston: 1968). For Vesey's revolt see John Lofton, *Insurrection in South Carolina* (Yellow Springs, Ohio: Antioch Press, 1964), and the *Trial Record of Denmark Vesey* (Beacon paperback, 1970). The North and South Carolina Narratives of the *American Slave*, cited above, were also drawn upon for this chapter.

5/Before the Wind

This chapter is based almost exclusively upon *A Narrative of the Life and Adventures of Henry Bibb, An American Slave, Written by Himself*, cited above. John F. Bayliss, ed., *Black Slave Narratives* (New York: Collier paperback, 1970); and Charles H. Nichols, *Many Thousand Gone* (Bloomington: Indiana University Press paperback, 1969) are useful introductions to slave narratives published before the outbreak of the Civil War.

6/The Selling of Solomon

Northup's work is unique among the narratives of ex-slaves. It constitutes the principal source upon which this chapter is based. *Twelve Years A Slave*, cited above, has an excellent introduction by Sue Eakin and Joseph Logsdon.

7/Behold, This Dreamer Cometh

Garrison's July 4 address, "The Dangers of the Nation," delivered at the Park Street Church, Boston, in 1829, is reproduced in John Anthony Scott ed. *Living Documents in American History* (New York: Washington Square Press, 1964; hardcover and paperback). McDuffie's rejoinder, under the title "Message on the Slavery Question," is reproduced in the same place. Garrison's *Thoughts on African Colonization*, originally published in 1834, has been reissued (Arno Press, New York: 1968). There is a full-scale study of the colonization movement: F. J. Staudenraus, *American Colonization Movement 1816–65* (New York: Columbia University Press, 1961).

8/Death, Without Benefit of Clergy

The Story of Theodore Weld is told in Benjamin P. Thomas, *Theodore Weld, Crusader for Freedom* (New Brunswick, N.J.: Rutgers University Press, 1950); that of Lovejoy in Merton Dillon, *Elijah Lovejoy, Abolitionist Editor* (Urbana, Illinois: University of Illinois Press, 1961). The principal primary source for this chapter, Edward Beecher, *Narrative of Riots at Alton* was first published in 1838 and reissued as a paperback with a fine introduction by Robert Merideth (New York: Dutton Paperback, 1965).

9/Unreasonable Seizures

For the initial Northern reaction to the abolitionists, see Lorman Ratner, *Powder Keg: Northern Opposition to the Antislavery Movement 1831–40* (New York: Basic Books, 1968). A fundamental study of the Liberty Laws and of the struggles that centered around them still remains to be written. The Supreme Court decision in Prigg's case is to be found in the Supreme Court reports, 16 Peters 539. Useful background material for the case is provided by Edward Raymond Turner, *The Negro in Pennsylvania* (1910. Reissued by Negro Universities Press, New York: 1969). For a clear and systematic statement of the rights of the accused in common law criminal procedure, see

Lloyd I. Paperno and Arthur Goldstein, *Criminal Procedure in New York* (Massapequa Park, N.Y.: Acme Book Co., 1960).

10/Rule or Ruin

The background to the 1850 crisis, arising out of the Mexican War, is provided by Milton Meltzer's fine study, *Bound for the Rio Grande* (New York: Alfred A. Knopf, Inc., 1974). John C. Calhoun's March 4, 1856 speech to the United States Senate is reproduced in John Anthony Scott, ed., *Living Documents in American History*, vol. I, cited above. Margaret Coit's *John C. Calhoun, American Portrait* (1950. Reissued as a Sentry paperback, Boston: Houghton Mifflin, 1961) is a well-written biography, sympathetic to its subject. For the text of the Fugitive Slave Act of 1850 and the verbatim record of the trial of Castner Hanway see James J. Robbins, *Report of the Trial of Castner Hanway for Treason in the Resistance of the Execution of the Fugitive Slave Law of September, 1850* (1852. Reissued by Negro Universities Press, Westport, Conn.: 1970).

11/Do As You Would Be Done By

There have been many attempts at biographies of Harriet Beecher Stowe, but easily the best introduction to the woman and her family is Lyman Beecher, *Autobiography* (1864. Reissued in two volumes by the Belknap Press of Harvard University, Cambridge, Mass.: 1961); and her own autobiographical novel, *Oldtown Folks* (1869. Reissued by same publisher, 1966.) Important clues to Harriet Stowe's theology are provided in Robert Merideth's brilliant study of Edward Beecher, *The Politics of the Universe: Edward Beecher, Abolition, and Orthodoxy* (Nashville: Vanderbilt University Press, 1968). *Uncle Tom's Cabin* is available in various paperback editions (Washington Square Press, Signet, Dolphin, Perennial). Indispensable also for the study and understanding of Mrs. Stowe's most famous work is her addition to it—*A Key to Uncle Tom's Cabin* (1853. Reissued by Arno Press, New York: 1969).

Useful commentary upon Mrs. Stowe will be found in Edmund Wilson, *Patriotic Gore* (New York: Oxford University

Press, 1962; Galaxy paperback, 1966); and Constance Rourke, *Trumpets of Jubilee* (1927. Reissued as a Harbinger Book, New York: Harcourt Brace and World Inc., 1963). Joseph Chamberlain Furnas, *Goodbye to Uncle Tom* (New York: W. Sloane Associates, 1956) presents a picture of Mrs. Stowe in many ways the antithesis of the one offered in this chapter.

12/Outer Darkness

Anthony Burns is the subject of a gripping narrative by Charles Emery Stevens, *Anthony Burns: A History* (1856. Reissued by Corner House Publishers, Williamstown, Mass.: 1973). The history of the Missouri Compromise is the subject of a definitive treatment by Glover Moore, *The Missouri Controversy 1819–21* (Lexington: University of Kentucky Press, 1953). For the struggle over Kansas, seen from sharply differing viewpoints, see Samuel A. Johnson, *The Battle Cry of Freedom* (Lawrence, Kansas: University of Kansas Press, 1954); and Alice Nichols, *Bleeding Kansas* (New York: Oxford University Press, 1954).

The Louisiana Purchase in all its wild beauty, as Dred Scott saw it, is shown in George Catlin's paintings: see Harold McCracken, *George Catlin and the Old Frontier* (New York: Dial Press, 1959). The Dred Scott decision will be found in the Supreme Court reports, 19 Howard 393. No definitive modern text of this case, giving concurring opinions and dissents, is available. For an abridged edition see Stanley J. Kutler, *The Dred Scott Decision: Law or Politics?* (Boston: Houghton Mifflin Co., 1967; paperback). For background facts, but with little fundamental analysis, see Vincent Charles Hopkins, *Dred Scott's Case* (1951. Reissued 1967, New York: Franklin Watts, Inc., and as a paperback by Atheneum.) There is a full-scale biography of Roger B. Taney by Carl Brent Swisher (1935. Reissued by Archon Books, Hamden, Conn.: 1961).

13/The Multitudinous Seas

The Lincoln-Douglas Debates are reproduced in Paul M. Angle, ed., *Created Equal? The Complete Lincoln-Douglas Debates of*

1858 (Chicago: University of Chicago Press, 1958); there is also a paperback edition, Robert Johannsen, ed., *The Lincoln-Douglas Debates of 1858* (New York: Oxford University Press, 1971). There are biographies of Douglas by Robert Johannsen and also by Gerald Capers, *Stephen A. Douglas Defender of the Union* (Boston: Little, Brown, 1959). For Lincoln, the abridgement of Carl Sandburg's multivolume biography is to be recommended (New York: Dell Publishing Co., 1959; hardcover and paperback, 3 vols.).

An interesting introduction to John Brown in his own words and in the judgments of contemporaries and subsequent historians is provided by Richard Warch and Jonathan Fanton, eds., *John Brown* (Englewood, N.J.: Prentice-Hall, 1973; paperback.) Other source material on John Brown includes *The Life, Trial and Execution of Captain John Brown* (1859. Reissued by Da Capo Press, New York: 1969); and Louis Ruchames, ed., *A John Brown Reader* (New York: Abelard-Schuman, 1959. Reissued as a paperback *John Brown: The Making of a Revolutionary*. New York: Grosset and Dunlap, 1969). For an account of the Harper's Ferry uprising, see Allan Keller, *Thunder at Harper's Ferry* (Englewood, N.J.: Prentice-Hall, 1958). Recent biographies of Brown have been written by Stephen B. Oates (New York: Harper and Row, 1970); Jules C. Abels (New York: The Macmillan Co., 1971); Nelson Truman (New York: Holt Rinehart and Winston Inc., 1972); and Richard O. Boyer (New York: Alfred A. Knopf, Inc., 1973).

INDEX

Brown, Julia, quoted, 60–61
Buchanan, James, 237, 241, 243, 246; quoted, 242
Buckingham, James, 38, 39; quoted, 26, 28, 38
Burns, Anthony, 195, 221
Butler, John, 10
Butler, Major Pierce, 5, 6, 7, 8, 22, 31, 99, 198
Butler, Mrs. Pierce, see Kemble, Fanny
Butler, Pierce, 10, 20, 22
Butler Island, 8, 10, 13, 16, 19, 53, 67, 73; map, 11

Calhoun, John C., 184, 186, 190, 191, 192, 220, 226; quoted, 186, 187–188, 189, 190, 191, 192; secession advised by, 192, 193, 220; on sectional equilibrium, 187–189
California, 182, 183, 184, 193, 228, 246; admitted to Union, 193; gold discovered in, 183
Canada, 92, 97, 98, 100, 102, 172, 216
Carlisle, Edmund, 69
Cass, Lewis, 182
Chaffee, Joseph, 231, 236
Charles, Samuel, 214
Charleston, S.C., 31, 68, 72
Chicago Press and Tribune, 249
Christiana, Pa., 197, 200
Cincinnati, 97, 98, 114, 146, 164, 205, 206, 208, 210, 211, 213, 214, 215
Civil rights movement, 127, 170
Civil War, 1, 10, 26, 108, 126, 172, 263, 271
Clark, Ann, 40
Clay, Henry, 183–184, 193
Cobb, Jeremiah, 85
Colonization Society, 130, 154
Colorado, 226
Common Sense (Paine), 220

Compromise of 1850, 193–194
Confederate States of America, 263
Confessions of Nat Turner (Gray), 73
Confessions of Nat Turner (Styron), 84
Connecticut Valley, 202
Constitution, 5, 8, 22, 175, 187, 236, 238, 240, 242, 256, 257, 267; and Bill of Rights, 171; fugitive slave clause in, 99, 100, 109, 166, 190
Constitutional Convention, 5, 6, 7
Copland, John, 261
Coppie, Edwin, 261
Corn crop, 45–46
Cotton, 7, 8, 41–42, 44; black-seed, 25; green-seed, 25; "scraping," 42; as South's dominant crop, 26, 41; graph of production, 27
Cotton gin, invention of, 25
Cousar, James H., 88
Covey, and Douglass, 57
Cumby, Green, 69

Davison, Elige, quoted, 34
Declaration of Independence, 7, 89, 132, 219, 252, 253–254, 256, 258
Deep South, 34, 38, 88, 102
Delaware, 88, 187, 188
Demby, murder of, 55, 57
Democratic party, 182, 226, 246, 247
District of Columbia, 184, 194
Douglas, Stephen, 193, 226, 229, 247; in debates with Lincoln, 248–249, 251–254, 256–258; quoted, 249, 251, 252, 253
Douglass, Frederick, 55, 57, 68, 69, 270; quoted, 57, 64
Dred Scott decision, 230, 236,

New Orleans, 31, 36, 114
New York City, 164
New York Semi-Weekly Post, 247
New York State, 104, 235, 236;
    and Act of 1840, 170–171
North Carolina, 36, 95
North Dakota, 226
Northup, Henry, 124
Northup, Joseph, 109
Northup, Mintus, 109
Northup, Solomon, 42, 44, 46,
    57, 109, 110, 111, 120, 121,
    122, 125, 166, 170, 270; and
    Bass, 124; as kidnap victim,
    109, 111–112, 114; quoted, 23,
    42, 44, 45, 46, 58, 111, 114,
    115, 116, 117, 119, 120, 121;
    as slave, 116–117, 119, 124

"Oh, Freedom" (song), 105–107
Ohio, 98, 99, 100, 102, 206, 235,
    244
Ohio River, 23, 26, 36, 92, 97,
    164
Old South, 34
Olmsted, Frederick Law, 31, 32,
    34, 53, 54; quoted, 31, 32, 34,
    54
Orleans (brig), 114

Paine, Tom, 220
Parker, James W., 83
Parker, William, 197
Patterson, Delicia, 58; quoted, 58
Paulding, James K., 38; quoted,
    38
Pennsylvania, 168, 172, 235
Pennsylvania Act of 1826, 168,
    170, 171, 172, 173; struck
    down by Supreme Court, 174–
    175
Philadelphia, 5, 8, 10, 19, 99, 164
Philanthropist, 164, 206
Phillips, Ulrich B., 51
Pierce, Dr., 198; quoted, 198

Pinelanders, of Georgia, 28, 30
Polk, James, 180
"Poor Rosy" (song), 64–66
Porter, Harriet, 205
Prigg, Edward, 173, 174
Prigg v. Pennsylvania, 173, 175,
    176, 190, 194, 230, 232, 237

Quakers, 218

Realf, Richard, 259
Republican party, 183, 244, 246,
    247, 249, 253, 263
Revolutionary War, 23, 78
Rio Grande, 26, 179
Runaways: advertisements for, 87,
    88; from border states, 88, 89;
    from Deep South, 88, 89; and
    fugitive slave law, 166–167; and
    liberty laws in free states, 168,
    170, 171, 172, 175; and white
    patrols, 124; *see also* Slavery;
    Underground Railroad

Saint Louis, 149, 150, 151, 156,
    230, 231, 232
Saint Louis Observer, 150, 151
Sanford, John, 236
Scott, Dred (Sam Blow), 175,
    230, 231, 232, 235, 236, 238;
    see also Dred Scott decision
Scott, Judge, 233; quoted, 233,
    235
Scott, Winfield, 182
Scoville, Joseph, 184
Sectional equilibrium, Calhoun's
    concept of, 187–189
Selling of Joseph, The (Sewall),
    201
Sewall, Samuel, quoted, 201
Seward, William, 36, 50; quoted,
    37
Shadrach, funeral of, 20
Sims, Thomas, 216
Sinda, 73, 76; strike led by, 67

This is Tony Scott's third book in the *Living History Library*, of which he is general editor. A graduate of Oxford and Columbia Universities, he has taught at Amherst College and the Fieldston School, New York. Presently he is visiting professor of legal history at Rutgers University.

Mr. Scott helped organize the youth marches on behalf of school integration in 1958 and 1959. He hikes, bikes, plays tennis and guitar. Among the numerous books he has authored or edited are *The Ballad of America, Teaching for a Change*, and *Fanny Kemble's America*.